The Path to Authorship

LISTEN UP, WRITER

How *Not* to Write Like an Amateur

Write like a pro

Nikki Hanna

Nikki Hanna

Published by Patina Publishing
Tulsa, Oklahoma 74120

neqhanna@sbcglobal.net
www.nikkihanna.com

Copyright © 2019 by Nequita Hanna

IBSN: 978-0-9978141-3-2

Manufactured in the United States of America

Photography: Steven Michaels, Tulsa, Oklahoma
Cover Design: Jaycee DeLorenzo, Sweet 'N Spicy Designs

Contributors: Lhonda Harris, Tom Bush,
Donna Parsons, William Bernhardt, Melanie Corbin,
Damien Hartzell, Staci Mauney,
Julie Kimmel-Harbaugh

TABLE OF CONTENTS

INTRODUCTION

When I retired twelve years ago, I took the advice of experts to retire *to* something. That *something* was writing. I had no concept of the craft of writing and did not realize agents, publishers, and many readers would recognize my amateur status after reading only a few pages.

The approach to my first book, a memoir, was similar to that of most novice writers. I simply started writing. The result was that, ten years and eight published books later, I rewrote it. After years of taking courses on writing, attending writers conferences and workshops, and, ultimately, teaching writing, I was embarrassed to put that first edition on display with my other books.

Because my journey to writing well was so laden with hard lessons related to craft, technology, and publishing, I became obsessed with helping newbie writers avoid the pitfalls I experienced. A focus on teaching, coaching, and creating how-to books on writing emerged. This book is my third on writing and includes materials I developed as handouts for writing presentations and workshops. It targets details with which both rookie and some seasoned writers are unaware—areas where naiveté sabotages best efforts and, in some cases, makes writers vulnerable to those who would take advantage.

This book has the potential to move a novice writer from neophyte status to authorship so quickly that the aftershock is similar to that of entering a room and seeing a toddler vertical and walking for the first time. It also shows how experienced writers can add shine to their compositions. Use my advice when it is compatible with your goals, and ignore it when it is not. My wish for you, dear reader, is that you write well, find joy and purpose in the process, and revel in the outcome.

If you have any young friends who aspire to become writers, the second greatest favor you can do them is to present them with a copy of "the Elements of Style." The first greatest, of course, is to shoot them now, while they're happy.—Dorothy Parker

SECTION I

GIVING THE GIFT OF WRITING

Like the fact that not all talented musicians, singers, artists, and actors are famous, not all fabulous writers are famous. Not all well-executed books find a publisher, and not all published books deserve to be published. But we authors write anyway. As Bonnie Hearn Hill said, "We don't pick writing. Writing picks us."—The Writer magazine, August 2019.

Chapter 1

FINDING JOY AND PURPOSE IN WRITING

You will know you are doing what you were born to do when time passes and you don't realize it.*

An old Texas country and western singer, Jerry Jeff Walker, recorded a song about a cowboy who grew up in Eastern society but worked as a cowhand in Montana. His kin and girlfriend back East sent letters begging him to come home. When he didn't, they wrote, "You must be crazy out there." As he sat on his horse, looking out over a herd of cattle settling in the moonlight, he thought about how those folks back East had never seen the northern lights or been awed by an eagle on the wing. They had never experienced the Great Divide or heard old Camp Cookie sing. He decided *they* were crazy back there.

We writers are like that cowboy. We love and obsess over things others don't understand and are driven by a current of creativity that will not be denied. If this makes us crazy, so be it. There is joy and a sense of purpose to be found in what we do.

---

*Any unattributed quotes are those of the author.

A PASSION FOR WRITING

If my doctor told me I had only six months to live,
I wouldn't brood. I'd type a little faster.—Isaac Asimov

Only writers understand the passion for writing. When I'm working on a book—usually for a year or two at least—friends ask me, "Aren't you finished yet?" That's a reasonable question from their perspective. Most likely, they rarely do anything that takes years to complete. I don't know how to explain to them what it takes to write a book. Writers know that five years is not an unusual length of time.

What keeps us writers going is passion—a burning desire to create and a peculiar pleasure in the brutality of the process. Torturing ourselves with the rollercoaster of the stages of writing, we go from concluding what we wrote is trash to an occasional, overwhelming realization of our brilliance. This is a feeling so intense that when we write something grand, we take our fingers off our keyboards, lean back in our ergonomically correct chairs topped with pillows, thrust our fists into the air, and shout, "Y-E-E-S-S-S!"

Now that I have a number of published books, I can say, "I am an author." I carry my books around in the trunk of my car, autograph them, and give them away. If someone throws money at me, I take it, but that's not what I'm about.

I'm all about the writing—the creation. It is not an option. It's an obsession that churns like an unrelenting cyclone in my head. That storm drives me, and the end result makes the challenges worth enduring. Gloria Steinem said, "Writing is the only thing that, when I do it, I don't feel I should be doing something else." That's the kind of passion that carries me through.

It is the sharing of our creations that challenges writers. For many, a state of malcontent slithers in when sales don't live up to expectations. No matter how hard they try and how exceptional their books, authors are severely challenged to sell their creations. An inherent unfairness plagues the profession. Great books earn a few hundred dollars for writers while mediocre books earn millions. Luck and serendipity often have more influence than talent and effort. These challenges taught me many lessons.

I learned about reality, failure, and the emotional influences writing provokes. I learned about the variety of pathways to achievement and fulfillment through writing. I learned there is so much more to writing books than selling them and making money—that they have a purpose beyond their value in the marketplace. I learned writing is a gift to be shared, not necessarily sold. I learned why I write. I learned to find my niche and to stay in my lane while occasionally—strategically—dabbling in another. I learned how to balance aspirations with reasonable expectations. I learned how to find joy through writing.

A WRITER'S REALITY

First you're an unknown, then you write one book and you move up to obscurity.—Martin Myers

What is most likely to make writers crazy is the reality of their world, which conflicts with the dreams most of them harbor. As they chase the joy their passion offers, they must stare down reality and find their own sweet spot in the writing landscape. My story, which I tell in my speeches and writing workshops, reveals how I did just that.

All I heard from the writing community when I started writing was this fantasy: *If you can land an agent and a publisher, you can sell lots of books and make lots of money.* Or, *if you self-publish, you can sell lots of books and make lots of money.* Every conference or workshop I attended and every book I read on writing focused on selling books, making money, and becoming famous, which is the industry standard of success for a writer.

I initially bought into that premise and aspired to the success it promised. That meant I performed many functions I didn't enjoy, and they were not working. No matter what I did, I didn't sell lots of books. I sold only a few here and there even though I worked hard.

Eventually, a sense of failure invaded my psyche, and I became a frustrated, stressed-out writer driven to escape by watching "crazy cat" videos on YouTube. Sleepless nights were common. When I did sleep, I dreamed I had insomnia. Most of my writer compadres were swimming in the same sea of discontent. No matter how good we were or how hard we tried, no one sold lots of books.

Reality is tough to take. Facing it head-on requires the courage to accept harsh facts and apply enough rational thought to effectively relate information to personal situations. Consider this: I can go to the store and buy a picture frame with a handsome man's picture in it, take it home, and place it on my dresser, but that doesn't mean I have a boyfriend. We writers need to stay grounded in reality as we chase our dreams.

When I talk to writers about the reality of the writing world, I have a sense I'm throwing a brick through a window because success stories are widely touted and internalized.

Readers are also out of touch with reality. I've had many well-intended, naive souls encourage me by suggesting that Oprah might discover my book. This irritates me to no end, and I ask myself, "How hard do I slap this person?" The reality is that remarkable success stories, though highly publicized, are extremely rare.

THE REALITIES OF THE PUBLISHING BUSINESS: It's tough to make a living with writing, but newbie writers and the general public don't know that. While I lunched with a writers group, a recently widowed woman told me she had to write a book quickly and get it out because she needed the income. I didn't have the heart to embarrass her in front of her writer friends, so I didn't say it, but I thought, *Oh, honey, you are in for another heartbreak. And you need to get a job.*

I can't count the number of times someone who discovered I was a writer made a remark about me making lots of money. I don't, and neither do most writers. Author S. J. Perelman said, "The dubious privilege of a freelance writer is he's given the freedom to starve anywhere." This thought applies to more than freelance. Why? Because . . .

- One million books per year are published and around twenty-three million are on the market. (Bowker—U.S. Book Registry)

- Only one percent of authors make a living from these books. (*authorearnings.com*)

- Typically, writers make royalties of only two to five dollars per book (e-books earn even less), and that is before writers' expenses.

- The average self-published book sells 250 copies in its first year and, just maybe, with significant effort, 3,000 over the life of the book. (*Publishers' Weekly* and Kameron Hurley's *The Cold Publishing Equation*)

Most writers won't sell lots of books no matter how good they are or what they do. A writer may have a list of hundreds of potential buyers for his book, but half of them never read books. Most of the rest read only in their preferred genres. Furthermore, friends and relatives frequently expect a writer to give them a book. With a writer's royalties running at two to five dollars per book, he's not going to experience a significant income. Do the math.

Writing a book is a tough way to make money. And no one is paying the author for the time and money he spent creating it. Considering these facts, if a writer's goal is to make money, he needs to get a job. This sounds incredibly harsh, and I take no pleasure in saying it, but truth is often a cruel master. It can also be a writer's salvation once he uses reality to refocus and find a niche in writing that gives him joy and guarantees success. (It *can* happen.)

Reality is often a downer. But before you are helplessly discouraged by this information, consider what Jim Murray said. "Learn to write. Never mind the damn statistics. If you like statistics, become a CPA." Don't do that, but do read on. Solutions are coming, but first, a bit more reality. Flow with me here.

THE ODDS: The basic supply and demand principle applies to books. The ratio of writers to publishing opportunities is staggeringly unequal. An agent at a conference said that out of the thousands of submissions his office receives each year, he selects twelve. Agent Dr. Uwe Stender gets an average of fifty queries a day—18,000 a year—and rejects 99 percent of them (*The Writer* magazine, July 2019). Once a writer gets an agent, another layer of potential rejection begins as that agent searches for a publisher.

Competing for book sales is just as disheartening. I put the key words "memoir" and "Iowa" into Amazon's search engine to locate my memoir, *Out of Iowa—Into Oklahoma.* So many books were listed that the odds of anyone seeing mine, let alone buying it, were remote. A new book is not only competing for sales with a million other books published that year, but with the millions published in previous years. Competition is beyond intense. This means rejection is not a reflection of a writer's talent, but rather, a mathematical probability.

These are hard realities to accept. Let me be clear. I don't enjoy delivering these messages, and my intent is not to discourage writers from chasing their dreams. If you have a fire in your belly for selling books, go for it. I admire your spunk and applaud your drive. You are the bomb. And, no doubt, you have no chance of succeeding if you don't try. Wayne Gretzky said, "You miss one hundred percent of the shots you don't take." Just be certain your aspirations are the result of careful deliberation and not the result of someone else's definition of success. The good news is that there are many ways to achieve success through writing other than selling books.

DREAMS AND ACHIEVABILITY: Writers have a creative spirit that will not be denied. The expression of that—the gift of that—is the sweet spot a writer settles into once he determines success for himself. That is not what the industry tells us. It says we must sell books to be successful—to be real writers.

It takes moxie not to accept that. Ralph Waldo Emerson said, "To be yourself in a world that is constantly trying to make you something else is the greatest accomplishment." Avoid getting swept away by industry rhetoric. Find the mix of writing activities that works for you. Focus on those you are good at and that bring you joy. Buck up. Do your own thing, and deliver what only you can.

Which of these is the best advice? "You can do anything you want to do," or "Find what you were born to do, and do that." In the early tryouts for American Idol, some awful singers perform. No doubt, someone told them "You can do anything you want to do." Some contestants would have been better served if they had been told, "Discover what you were born to do, and do that." This doesn't mean they can't sing and enjoy it. Rather, it means they are not going to make a living at it.

Some dreams are not doable. This is difficult to hear, but for many writers, defining success as selling books, making money, and becoming famous is naive idealism squared. And, as in the entertainment and music industry, only the most talented, hardest working, *and luckiest* writers achieve success because of the odds and the fickleness of serendipity. Talent might have little to do with it.

This doesn't mean every writer cannot enjoy writing. Whatever his talent, he can, just as anyone can enjoy singing no matter their talent. Heck, I sing, and I cannot sing.

SHAPING THE DREAM

Steering away from the primary goal of selling books and making money is not giving up. It's finding your niche—your own unique path to joy and purpose through writing.

When a writer's aspirations are the result of his own ideas about success, rather than someone else's, the prospect of realizing them is substantially increased. The writer who shapes dreams around innate talent, realities of the writing world, and possibilities beyond fame and fortune is on the path to becoming a joyful writer. What is your writing dream? Ask yourself the following:

- Have you refused to let others define your dream for you?
- Is your dream based on an awareness of innate abilities and realistic outcomes?
- Is there a niche in the writing world that is compatible with your innate abilities?
- Can you discover reasons to write other than money and fame?
- Can you be content with selling "some" books as opposed to "a lot" of books?
- Can you consider what you write a gift to be shared rather than a money source?
- Can you find purpose in sharing your mind, spirit, and wisdom through what you create?

If you answered yes to those questions, you cannot fail. You will be successful and joyful. And none of those approaches to writing involve selling books and making money.

REDEFINING SUCCESS

You want to be a writer? Good for you. So does that guy. And that girl. And him. And her. And that old dude. And that young broad. And your neighbor. And your mailman. . . . an ocean of wannabe ink elves and word eaters. I don't say this to daunt you. Or to be dismissive. But you have to differentiate yourself.—Chuck Wendig

By differentiating himself, each writer finds his niche. This requires a healthy appreciation of where and how to fit into the teeming masses of writers. When I attended a writers conference in New York City with thousands of writers, the scale of the industry in which I aspired to become a player dawned on me.

I go to several writing conferences every year, and I often feel alone in a crowd, and for good reason. With the introduction of self-publishing, increasing numbers of aspiring writers are chasing the dream of fame and fortune. It took a mental shift for me to adjust to the reality that the supply of writers far exceeds the demand for them. Rather than give up on my writing dreams, I reassessed my outlook. After about five years of frustration, I discovered a fresh perspective—one that fulfilled me. As a result, I redefined success as follows:

I wrote it. I shared it. And some people enjoyed it.

That's it. That's all. With this definition, I could not fail. I was successful when the words flowed. The only way to fail was to quit. This promoted a fresh vision. Writing was no longer about selling books. It was about sharing. That perspective inspired me to add teaching writing to my repertoire, which changed everything. I discovered my niche and, as a result, became incredibly productive. After internalizing the concept of doing what I was born to do, I found both joy and purpose in writing.

- Writing became a gift to be shared. Selling became secondary.

- Unpleasant tasks were eliminated or minimized.

- My focus switched to the writing functions I enjoyed and was naturally good at.

- I became energized and more prolific.

- Writing became a job from which I didn't need a vacation.

- I became so happy I could have married myself.

With this fresh perspective, it occurred to me that *I may not be the best writer I know, but I might be the happiest.* I still dream, at times, of selling books and financial and professional success. Every writer is hungry on the inside. But I avoid writing processes that suck the joy out of me in order to experience that unlikely scenario. How do you define success? Redefine it in a way that guarantees joy in writing. Writer Kameron Hurley defines success simply as "staying in the game." Any writer can do that.

OPTIONS: How do you stay in the game? There are many avenues to finding joy in writing. If writing has you frustrated and is robbing you of joy, eliminate as many unenjoyable functions as you can. Explore adding those that give you pleasure. For example, I once designated Mondays as submission days. That was not a happy time. I hate doing submissions. I'd rather sort all my band-aids into one box or become a dirt-diva rock star and clean house than do submissions. When I stopped doing them, my house wasn't as clean, but Mondays became joyful again.

This perspective is not for every writer. If you are a publication enthusiast, don't be like me. Check out *Submittable*, *The Submission Grinder* (both free), *TheReviewReview.net*, *NewPages*, and *Duotrope* for online lists of submission opportunities.

Most writers are unaware of the broad spectrum of writing paths available to them and the multiple mental perspectives a writer can embrace. If you have an adversarial relationship with any function, consider eliminating it. If you suffer through book signings, consider not doing do them. If making a pitch to an agent triggers a flush like you've had too much merlot, perhaps you avoid them. If social media makes you feel as though your brain is being agitated by complex algorithms, you can avoid such online activities. Alternatives exist. Numerous writing opportunities are listed at the end of this chapter. However, if the drive to sell is a priority, take William Bernhardt's advice: "For every six hours you write, plan on spending two on the business of publishing and marketing."

Consider this vision: Your talent is a gift to be shared rather than a money source. Set your primary goal as: To share your mind, spirit, wisdom, and uniquely quirky self with others through writing. Tie your definition of success to that objective. You can do that and still strive to sell books and make money because you are not limited to your top priority.

Sharing requires courage. Because I'm humbled by other more-talented writers, and I recognize the limits of my expertise, I could choose not to share what I know. I could not write this book. But I celebrate what I do have to offer, and I put it out there. It's medicine to do so—to contribute.

The therapeutic value of writing is often under-appreciated. Writing changed my encore years. I learned my writing has purpose beyond its value in the marketplace. I learned writing is a gift that I should give generously. I learned why I write.

My wish for you, dear writer, is that you have a similar experience, that you find your passion and your niche in the world of writing, that you bask in the joy and purpose it fosters, and that you write something fabulous. So show off, you zany, marvelous writer. Write and be joyful.

****

ALTERNATIVE PATHS TO SUCCESS, JOY, AND PURPOSE

Writing Options:
- Enter writing contests.
- Blog.
- Do freelance work.
- Write a column in a newsletter or help publish one.
- Produce a family newsletter.
- Submit to anthologies (good odds of publication).
- Write memoir—yours or someone else's.
- Write stories or poems for birthdays, special occasions, and for condolences.
- Do readings at book clubs and other organizations, or host readings in your home. People love them.
- Submit to magazines or other publications.
- Attend writers conferences; network with other writers.
- Become active on social media.
- If you do one online thing, do a website.

Participate in the Writer Community:
- Collaborate with other writers.
- Find a writing tribe or create one.
- Join writers groups. Volunteer, or become an officer.
- Host critique events or writers socials in your home.
- Participate in writers colonies and retreats.
- Help organize writers events, conferences, book signings, and library events.
- Support local bookstores and libraries and volunteer to help with their events.
- Support other writers' work, read their books, sponsor book launches, and give reviews on Amazon.
- Coach, teach, and encourage novice writers.
- Edit, beta read, critique, and become an expert reviewer.

The writing fairy struck, and Wallis' brilliance exploded onto the page. He invented such words as understupid and cosmic doozy (payback). He labeled one character as a sweet, warm cup of love; and another, a whacked out, beastly, evil bastard. Metaphors and similes splatted onto pages. Emboldened by the courage of self-expression, he said, "If you don't like this simile, you won't like the next one." His writing shone like a soldier's boot, and the joy of writing washed over him. Be like Wallis.

Chapter 2

HOW *NOT* TO WRITE LIKE AN AMATEUR

When I write, I feel like an armless, legless man with a crayon in his mouth.—Kurt Vonnegut

Writing, if done right, is a complicated business, much more so than most novice writers realize. Once they figure that out, they relate to the above quote. Agents, publishers, or contest judges will evaluate a writer's work based on the quality of the craft. In contrast, readers may not notice or understand the details of professional writing, but they sense when good craft is missing. Whether any of this is important to you as a writer is a personal decision determined by your goals. If you aspire to sell what you write, mastery of craft and an understanding of the publishing industry are essential.

The publishing environment is intensely competitive. A writer cannot afford to come off as an amateur, and professionals will spot one in short order. It's imperative that a writer, eager to sell books, stands out by applying good craft. Many rookie writers don't know there is such a thing as writing craft and that, without it, submissions are headed for reject piles no matter how good the stories.

To get started on the path to awareness of craft, go over the list, "What Shouts *Amateur*," at the end of this chapter. It reveals the most obvious clues that a writer has not mastered craft. An expert will spot such situations in the first few pages, if not in the first sentence or paragraph. You may conclude such details are petty and that writing craft is an atrocity against humanity—worse than bad coffee—and you would be right. I have an inkling, though, if you are reading this book, you are up for the simmering details that make your writing stand out in a good way.

AUTHORSHIP

The person born with a talent they are meant to use will find their greatest happiness in using it.—Johann Wolfgang von Goethe

It's your call whether to aspire to become a professional writer or, instead, to write without worrying about that. Many writers have not published anything but have written for enjoyment since their youths. It is not unusual for such people to believe they're not writers. Studying craft may not be their thing, but this does not mean they are not writers. They are, even though they do not aspire to achieve the industry standard of success, which is to sell books, make money, and become famous. It is sad they believe they are not writers because, if you write, you are a writer. For those writers, craft may not be important, and that's okay. This is especially true in the case of memoir.

A flawed memoir has a charm all its own, one that reveals the essence of the subject of the memoir and the person writing it. It is more important a memoirist has a book than that he has a perfect one. Memoir trumps craft.

We all must find our own paths and define success on our own terms. Whatever approach you take to writing, know you are a writer because you write. Stephen King said, "Language does not always have to wear a tie and lace-up shoes."

THE PATH TO AUTHORSHIP: Whether a writer sells books or not, good craft demonstrates his commitment to his art and gives him writing muscles. When physical gestures are repeated, the memory of them is encoded in muscles. This is why we don't forget how to ride a bike. Writing is like that. Repeated writing creates writing muscles.

Craft is the path to *authorship*. Isn't that a lovely word? *Authorship*. What does it mean? Authorship means a writer displays the marks of an expert. It means inadequacies will not distract from what he creates. It means he embraces the craft of writing, including the trivial nuisances. It means he is bold and dares to confront barriers that obstruct the timid. It means he expresses himself with bravado, and his product is never trite. It means he produces quality work that demonstrates he is serious about being a writer—that he is a professional. It means he is generous with his talent.

Authorship requires that a writer be active in the writer community, participate in the profession, and understand the industry. (I keep up to date on such matters by attending conferences, subscribing to *The Writer* magazine, and following William Bernhardt's blogs, podcasts, workshops, and newsletters at the *Red Sneaker Writer Center.*)

APPRENTICESHIP: A writer who aspires to be a professional would do well to consider his early years as an apprenticeship and to embrace continuous learning—the key to solid writing craft. As you learn, self-confidence blossoms. I've been studying writing for over twelve years, and I'm still learning. I'm in my seventies. I figure by the time I'm ninety, I'll be a pretty good writer.

CONTINUOUS LEARNING— THE KEY TO AUTHORSHIP

Learn as if you will live forever.—Gandhi

Many a wannabe writer simply decides he wants to be a writer, and he writes something. There is nothing wrong with that. In fact, that's what an aspiring writer should do, even if he has not yet learned how to write well. After all, one way to learn how to write is to write. While doing so, though, a focus on learning is vital.

When I retired, I wrote a book. Ten years later, I rewrote it. I had come so far and become so much more proficient at writing craft that I could no longer share the book with pride. So I gave it new life. I value both versions of the book because the gap between them reflects how far I've come.

REWARDS FROM LEARNING: It's tough to find anything that produces more personal growth in any profession than learning. For over twelve years, I've taken writing classes, attended workshops, and gone on retreats. I've participated in critique sessions, attended writers conferences, and learned from editors. Those activities sparked a camaraderie with other writers that has been invaluable. And then, there is this:

> Learning is a gift you give yourself that lasts the rest of your life. When you learn something, it

becomes a part of you. You hold it forever. No one can ever take it away. Few things in life offer this measure of value. (This is a message worth sharing with children and grandchildren.)

That's not all. When you share what you learn, you give a forever gift to others, and that fosters a sense of purpose. Don't put off learning. Get all over it. Here's how:

- Write. Always write. Routinely exercise those writing muscles.

- Read. Always be reading something. Read in your genre and in other genres. Read good books and bad books. Stephen King suggests that bad books teach as much as good ones.

- Study writing. Take classes and workshops. Amazon and bookstores offer how-to books on writing. Some excellent ones are listed in the Appendix.

- Subscribe to *The Writer* magazine.

- Sit down, one-on-one, with your editor and go over suggested edits. Doing so is the most expedient way to learn.

- Join a writers group. Network the heck out of seasoned writers there. You'll learn and grow as a writer, and you stand a good chance of finding a mentor and a critique group.

- Take writing courses at educational institutions. These are often offered at low cost through adult learning programs.

- Attend writers conferences. Industry experts and successful authors are there. Pick a location you've always wanted to visit, google writers conferences and workshops at that location, and sign up for a writing vacation.

When you read the works of other writers and work with editors and proofreaders, you will often be humbled by their talent. Remember this: Your writing is your gift to give. Don't let someone else's rainbow outshine your own.

THE GENRE BOUNCE: A serious writer will explore writing in multiple genres. A good way to do this is to enter writing contests that have multiple genre categories with low word counts (including short stories, essays, poems, and articles). Writers who step outside their comfort zone will be surprised at how much their writing improves.

One of the most joyful times in my writing journey occurred when I focused on entering contests. I am mostly a nonfiction writer. When I studied fiction and poetry so I could be competitive in contests, my nonfiction writing blossomed. I call this *the genre bounce*. Incorporating principles of other genres into my writing gave me an edge. This resulted in a winning streak in contests, and it thrust my work into a wonderland of creative expression. I found myself tap dancing into the realm of authorship.

From fiction, I learned about structure, plot, pace, transitions, tension, conflict, dialogue, creating curiosity, character development, setting descriptions, climax, resolution, and a host of other writing principles that rounded out my portfolio of writing skills.

From poetry, I learned about phrasing, flow and rhythm, articulating emotions more deeply, using extraordinarily expressive words, effective word arrangement, and clever techniques, such as ending sentences with a strong word.

Screenwriting fosters a genre bounce as writers learn to tell a story strictly from sound and what is shown on a screen rather than from narrative.

With all this awareness, I became a writing rock-star aficionado, at least in my mind. I knew some stuff, and that felt good. I'm not brave enough to pursue a genre bounce from horror, thriller, adventure, fantasy, sci-fi, or the paranormal, though. I fear the influences of the mystical. Given my firm grip on reality, fanciful stories are outside my wheelhouse. A demon, unicorn, or submarine popping up in one of my pieces is unlikely to work for me or my audience, although I can imagine a robot happening—sort of, maybe.

The romance genre is also off the table. For me, reading or writing such a passionate book would be like searching for bath oil in a farm implement store. I'd write something strikingly stupid like: "He took her hand, brought it to his lips, and then kissed his own hand."

Contemplating reading or writing in such categories isn't so scary that it sends me to *Chicken-Soup-for-the-Soul* territory, but it does make me wish Erma Bombeck were still alive to inspire my humorous prose. Nevertheless, I am in awe of those talented enough to write with such creative imagery and whimsical sorcery. When observing them, I'm like an outdoor dog peering through the screen door at a cat and feeling like an anti-pet.

I apologize for that tirade. The genre bounce thing got away from me.

BREAKING WRITING RULES: Writers are generally forgiven for breaking rules when they do it intentionally and intelligently, especially when done to avoid restraints on creativity. Don't be restricted by convention if it obstructs expression. It's not as though you violate a rule and a grammar fairy dies. An example of this is using short, incomplete sentences (called fragments) for stylistic effect. Readers and writing experts are quick to pick up on such intentional violations and are okay with them. Here are two rules I broke to achieve my writing goals.

Data Dumps: Fiction writers are taught not to data dump, which involves unleashing a bunch of descriptive information all at once. Ideally, such details should be introduced in small chunks throughout the manuscript so they don't interrupt the forward flow of the story. Sometimes, though, especially in memoir, a writer requires several pages to describe his room as a child, his grandfather, or his hometown. Such data dumps are acceptable as long as they are captivating.

In my book, *Red Heels and Smokin'*, a story-like memoir, I took several pages to describe differences between the rural culture in Iowa and the one in Oklahoma. This information was important because it set the stage for conveying how I coped with cultural shifts, which was the central theme of the book.

Although country boys grew on me like mold in a shower, the significance of the difference between a staid and true Iowa farm boy and a wild and rowdy Oklahoma cowboy was profound. This is illustrated in the "Example of a Data Dump" at the end of this chapter.

Preaching: I also broke the memoir/nonfiction rule not to preach. The target audience in my memoir, *Out of Iowa—Into Oklahoma,* was family. One of my goals for writing the book was to share life's lessons with my children, grandchildren, and future descendants. The dilemma of how to do that without being preachy was solved by listing short, bulleted "Lessons Learned" in the Appendix. This allowed me to share wisdom while avoiding pontification in the body of the memoir. I was old and well-seasoned, so there were many lessons— so many that one reader asked, "Is there any karaoke in there?" I interspersed humorous lessons throughout the list to entice readers to get through all of them while searching for laughs:

- Don't pack vibrating toys in luggage when traveling by plane.

- When a baby's hand is in the way during an ultrasound, it's a boy.

- If you swear in front of children, don't follow up with, "Oh, shit."

- If a man is quiet, don't assume he's mysterious. He may just be stupid.

- Don't ask older people how they feel unless you really want to know.

- March Madness is not a sale at Macy's.

- Stay away from people with guns who are looking for their anti-depressants.

It's unlikely a publisher would allow such a deviation from the norm. Self-publishing gave me the freedom to express myself with abandon and to share wisdom without intruding on the text. Feedback from readers suggests the lessons learned were a hit. I didn't think of nieces and nephews as my audience as I wrote the memoir, but learned after publication that this lessons learned list was a hit with them.

Hint: To minimize preaching, identify preachy comments and rewrite them. Search for such words as *must, should, need to, do not, don't, cannot, can't, never,* and *absolutely.*

I subscribe to the suggestion that adverbs be used sparsely, perhaps two or three to a book. However, I consistently break the rule not to stack adjectives. I layer them on. Each writer's style is determined by his willingness to express himself in unique ways, which is what creativity is all about. Be bold. Put your mark on your creations while not being such a maverick that you turn off publishers, editors, or your audience. And avoid expressing your rebel spirit in the first few pages of a story where you want to demonstrate your mastery of craft.

TRENDS IN WRITING CRAFT: Rules of craft are sometimes controversial, and they evolve over time. For example, semicolons (with compound sentences) are as unpopular as feral cats these days. And it is now preferred to use only one space after a period at the end of a sentence instead of two. If you are using two, you are not trendy, like if you still have a landline. The Oxford comma (the one before *and/or* in the last of a series) fell out of favor in the seventies and is now back. Agents and publishers generally appreciate writers who are up on industry trends.

I learned to punctuate in the 1960s. Recognizing that punctuation requirements had changed since then, I asked several young technological geniuses at the Apple store, "How do you use commas these days?"

One said, "No one uses commas anymore."

Another suggested, "Just don't use commas stupid."

The next one said, "Put a comma where you would pause when you speak."

Then—the *pièce de résistance*—a social network aficionado said, "Just use a happy face."

The young geniuses were no good to me at all on the matter of punctuation.

Since *whom* and *shall* are rarely used in conversation these days, many publishers are okay with using *who* and *will* all the time. Also, editors rarely get in a wad over a split infinitive these days, unless the writer is engaged in academic writing. And starting a sentence with the conjunctions *and*, *but*, *so*, and *yet* is now generally accepted —just don't overdo. Dangling participles, on the other hand, are still in disfavor, as well they should be.

Beyond the bounds of good writing is bad writing, which involves such things as unleashing flurries of adverbs, failing to kill one's darlings, using prepositions improperly, or misspelling *Tijuana*. Writers who deliver such faux pas are not necessarily rebels. Many are just confused or overwhelmed, like the frustrated little boy who ended a sentence with four prepositions: "What are you bringing that book I don't want to be read out of up for?"

There are writers who get drunk on writing and pontificate, embellish, and write with obnoxious literary flourish. Then, there are the rebel souls determined to use bad craft as a blatant act of defiance. However, most sloppy craft happens because writers rush to birth something and skip the editing process. This results in bad writing, such as these examples:

- Ed panicked and turned when he heard a low, menacing noise coming from his rear.

- Suddenly, the door opened slowly.

- The most common side-effect of a sleep drug is sleep.

- When Ike Turner died, a newspaper headline said, "Ike Turner Beats Tina to Death."

I apologize for those. My humor frequently meanders into the arena of overkill, but you get the point.

FINDING YOUR SWEET SPOT

A professional writer is an amateur who didn't quit. — Richard Bach

Once a writer realizes all that writing requires, he might be tempted to abandon it. Rather than quitting, consider yourself the only audience, and write for yourself. Enjoy the freedom of that. You may find yourself rebounding and getting back into the game.

No one can promise you fame and fortune—that's a tough gig to land in this business—but odds are, you'll find your happy when you find your niche. This can be life-changing and seductive because it offers a plethora of rewards. Treat yourself as though you are what you aspire to become. Seek your sweet spot in the writing world. Express yourself fiercely. Be a joyful, unapologetic scribe, one who is elegant in his weirdness. Seduce with fabulous words written well and with aplomb. Be that person.

****

WHAT SHOUTS *AMATEUR*

Issues Usually Obvious in the First Few Pages:
- Literary showing off (big words and flourish), such as *we made our departure* instead of *we went home*

- Two spaces after a period at the end of sentences

- Page numbers or headers and footers on blank pages

- Unnecessary words (professionals write economically)

- Periods and commas outside of quotation marks

- Overuse of *would* or *had* (suggests verb tense issues)

- Underlining, excessive italics, and boldface in fiction

- Inappropriate or overuse of exclamation marks. Never use more than one in a row. Don't use merely to make a point. Use only for surprise, excitement, shouting, or strong emotion

- Formatting issues, such as inconsistent setup or widows. (A widow is a single word on a line at the end of a paragraph or a single line at the beginning or end of a page.)

- Overuse of front and back matter and misspelling *foreword* or *copyright* (see Chapter 10 - "Parts of a Book")

Writing Craft Issues:
- Lack of voice (nothing distinctive about the writing)

- Triteness (stating the obvious—what reader already knows)

- Flat characters—under developed, lacking emotion

- Absence of setting descriptions or poor or intrusive ones

- Too much telling rather than showing

- Too much passive, rather than active, voice

- Overuse of adverbs and adjectives

- Use of clichés and excessive or unskilled use of similes and metaphors

- Data dumping (too much description/exposition at once that interrupts flow and causes readers to skip parts)

- Not applying point-of-view techniques

- Use of opaque words: *very, really, pretty, literally, actually, basically, just, even, all, rather, quite, truly*

- Overuse of empty words: *they, them, there, this, it, items, things* (use more descriptive words where possible)

- Excessive use of *that, the, any, a lot, now, then, still, yet, well, get, got, must*

- Awkward transitions and unorganized structure

- Unfortunate use of dialogue tags, especially with adverbs

- Out of order sentences or redundant ones in paragraphs

- No scene breaks when point of view, time, or setting change

Writing Mechanics—Grammar, Punctuation, Spelling:
- Misspelled words

- Improperly punctuated compound or complex sentences

- Improper or inconsistent application of tense or person

- Improper subject-verb agreement

- Incomplete (fragmented) sentences when not done stylistically (judges and publishers can tell)

- Semicolons (out of favor when joining two sentences)

- Not using the Oxford comma

- Spaces before or after hyphens or dashes

EXAMPLE OF A DATA DUMP

In general, a data dump is a bad idea, especially in an early chapter of a book where it slows the flow. However, in my memoir, *Red Heels and Smokin'*, the cultural differences between Iowa and Oklahoma needed explanation for the story to make sense. So I data dumped.

Raised on a farm in a small Iowa community, the enforced conformity of the heartland shaped me. With strong northern European influences, no one in Iowa showed emotion over religion or anything else. Strict adherence to societal norms was required. Diversity didn't exist. Stability was paramount; and adventuresome spirits, stymied. Iowans denounced rebels and high rollers. Integrity was compulsory in all quarters. At that time, divorce in the heartland was rare and hugely scandalous. These Iowa cultural characteristics contrasted sharply with Oklahoma's wild and rowdy nature.

When I came to Oklahoma in the 1960s, Tulsa was known as the Oil Capital of the World. Blond, manicured, bejeweled women in Mercedes cruised the streets. Thriving steak restaurants and private clubs catered to oilmen in starched shirts, seam-pressed Levi jeans, gleaming belt buckles, gold jewelry, and blazers. Downtown bustled with an abundance of cultural events financed by wealthy oilmen. Lively music venues and rollicking clubs produced a severe in-congruency because Oklahoma was an evangelistic haven—and it was *dry*. A person had to fill out forms to get an alcoholic drink. The state also had the second highest divorce rate in the country after Nevada.

Oklahoma's history is unique. In the late 1800s and early 1900s, neighboring states nourished a white, Anglo-Saxon, protestant, midwestern culture. Farmers built white farmhouses, large red barns, and a multitude of sturdy outbuildings. In contrast, Oklahoma bore the markings of Indian Territory. Bleak landscapes—peppered with tents, trading posts, and lean-to houses—were populated by Indians, outlaws, and Civil War refugees. Then, the land runs in 1889 introduced homesteaders.

Oklahoma finally achieved statehood in 1907. Next, the oil boom hit with a fury. That brought in the railroad, which changed everything. Neighborhoods of ostentatious mansions sprang up, and Tulsey Town became the city of Tulsa. During this time, the community projected an inauthentic impression that all was well. It wasn't. Underneath its image, intolerance smoldered, and in 1921, festering Southern leanings fostered the worst race massacre in the history of the country.

Art deco was fashionable during the oil boom, and it was broadly reflected in the city's architecture, as opposed to the Federal and European styles popular in cities in surrounding states. The contrast between a brash oilman mentality and an extreme evangelistic one was illustrated when one businessman touted the art deco influences and another responded, "Jesus loves art deco."

Jesus must have loved oil as well because Oklahoma thrived. Over time, though, the petroleum industry faltered. Today, Oklahoma is more like surrounding agricultural states, and Southern influences produce redneck, macho, good-old-boys in feed store caps, who still believe in the beer fairy. The juxtaposition of a down-home, evangelical persona with the materialistic influences from the oil era causes the state to suffer from a personality disorder. It's as though *Saturday Night Live's* church lady and Michael Douglas' greedy character in *Wall Street* had a baby. Then Jed Clampett shot at a rabbit and struck oil.

Because of my tightly structured, traditional Iowa upbringing, nothing in Oklahoma made sense when I moved there in 1966, but I liked it. I liked it a lot.

SECTION II

AUTHORSHIP—
WRITING PRINCIPLES

Never, ever use repetitive redundancies.

Don't use no double negatives.

Proofread carefully to see if you any words out.

—William Safire

Chapter 3

CRAFT—THE PATH TO AUTHORSHIP

I hate commas in the wrong places.—Walt Whitman

A counselor asked a little boy whose parents were getting divorced, "Tucker, are you overwhelmed with all that's going on?" The boy hesitated for a moment, squinted his eyes, pursed his lips, and then responded excitedly, "Yes! Yes! I have too many whelms!"

Craft can make a writer feel as though he has too many whelms. He might even conclude that craft is a nuisance, and he'd be right. It's hard to get excited about the prickly and less creative aspects of writing. If you are considering whether to go down the path of studying writing, remember this: Craft is what sets you apart. It demonstrates your commitment to your art and gives you writing muscles. Craft is what keeps you from writing like an amateur. If you've concluded craft is not important, listen up.

Marcia Riefer Johnston, author of *Word Up,* suggests that those who are impressed by the mastery of craft are the same people with the power to hold you back—a contest judge, an agent, a publisher, or a reader who posts a review.

Stephen King, in his book, *On Writing,* disputes the idea that grammar is "a pain in the ass." Instead, he proposes that it's what gets your thoughts up on their feet and walking.

Craft is tedious, and executing it well is a never-ending process. I've been studying writing intensely for twelve years and didn't know, until recently, that if I used a noun as a verb, or vice versa, I would go to Dante's Hell. This surprise convinced me I had a symbiotic relationship with ignorance, so I was tempted to move on to Plan B, which involved deciding I didn't care about such minute details. In such situations, I've been known to take my marbles and go home.

This experience suggests an important message. Craft can cause you to give up. Don't do that. When the low points overwhelm—and they will—sip on an impertinent merlot and write something weird. As I've said before, it is more important you write something than that you write it perfectly. Many quotes, even from experts, have something wrong with them, such as a *which* that should be *who*, an *in to* that should be *into*, a split infinitive, or a dangling participle. Even books written by established writers and published by major publishers are plagued with craft issues. This is a testament to the challenges and complications of applying writing craft.

Not only is the writing a challenge, the execution processes (revision, editing, and proofreading) are so complex that they sabotage any hope of perfection. There are two messages here: (1) You will never get the perfect book, but you should try, and (2) You will be in good company when you don't get it. Even so, know that mastering writing craft is the path to becoming a professional writer.

WHAT'S IN IT FOR YOU? It is because craft is thorny and loaded with brutal details that mastering it builds self-esteem, promotes a sense of pride, and makes a writer more competitive. Additionally, when a person knows he is good—really good—at something as challenging as craft, he achieves a level of self-confidence that propels him toward lofty ambitions and accomplishments.

A comprehensive compilation of craft details is beyond the scope of this book; however, tips in the Appendix reveal helpful approaches to writing that have the potential to thrust a writer forward quickly along the continuum from amateur to professional.

Let me qualify this perspective. The extent to which a writer embraces craft is a personal choice based on goals and aspirations. If studying, researching, and learning are objectionable to you, and you're not interested in publishing, don't let craft requirements slow your roll. Walk your own path to finding joy and purpose in writing.

CRAFT—A MEASURE OF PROFESSIONALISM

Craft is the background that makes your brilliance pop.

Craft is a fundamental ingredient for writing expertise. Writing experts recognize the quality of craft immediately. A contest judge said, "I usually know within the first couple of paragraphs if I have a winner." Writing is not something you do, and it's done. If done well, writing requires multiple drafts of a manuscript and many iterations of review, with each revision adding another layer of polish.

DELIVER THE EXTRA: Writing something ordinary is the most serious mistake a writer can make. It is equivalent to a deadly Mexican dinner—tasty during the meal but lethal afterward. A writer needs to be endlessly resourceful at distinguishing himself. His writing must stand out from the masses. Otherwise, he offers his audience nothing of value. The rest of this chapter and the upcoming ones on "Revision, Editing, and Proofreading" and "Voice, Style, and Humor" include methods, processes, and tools that ensure a writer expresses himself in unique and captivating ways.

CATEGORIES OF CRAFT: I apologize for going all textbook on you here, but you need to know this. There are three categories of craft:

> **(1) Rules:** These include proper grammar, spelling, punctuation, word use, sentence structure, writing technique, and such mechanics as formatting and presentation.

> **(2) Preferences of Experts:** These requirements aren't necessarily right or wrong. In fact, many are controversial, but experts care about them. They include such things as avoiding adverbs, using only one space at the end of a sentence, whether its okay to start a fiction story with a quote, applying the Oxford comma, and whether to capitalize *Internet.* It's best to go with what's trending with publishers.

> **(3) The Finesse of Writing:** This includes expert-level writing techniques and craft practices, such as show, don't tell; active voice; optimal syntax (word use and order); and expert structural design.

Don't put off learning. Get all over it. The following pages and the Appendix will put you well on the path to mastering the craft of writing and achieving authorship.

CRAFT AND READER EXPECTATIONS

One of the most devastating mistakes a writer
can make is to write something that is trite.

When coaching novice writers, my goal is to make them aware of the basics of writing craft in just two sessions. We go over my red-lined critique of their first chapters in the second session. Usually, these manuscripts bleed with red markings. So I warn them: "After we review this chapter, you'll need to go home and heal because I'm going to hit you with everything I've got." They do heal, because, in the first session, I invested considerable time convincing them that craft matters, and that mastering it would make them more successful.

What writers learn from these first-chapter critiques can be applied throughout their manuscripts. The result is polish that keeps them from appearing amateurish.

Writers must nail the basic principles of craft to get published, but that is not enough. In the competitive publishing environment, successful writers must not only demonstrate mastery of writing practices and principles, they must distinguish themselves in creative ways, such as through voice and style. These expressive components of writing craft are paramount when striving to capture the attention of agents, publishers, or judges, as well as readers.

THE PROMISE: Readers have expectations. When you put what you write out into the world, you make a promise to them that what you created is worthwhile. Readers recognize good writing instantly. They also know bad writing when they see it—instantly. They may have difficulty figuring out what's wrong, but they know when something is off. To be successful, writers are obliged to make every sentence interesting and tell readers things they don't already know. It seems I should not have to tell writers this, but I frequently read manuscripts, blogs, and contest entries that don't do that.

Successful writers surprise readers. What they write about, and how they say it is out of the ordinary and captivating. Otherwise, the writer is like poet Dylan Thomas, who said, "Someone is boring me. I think it's me." Don't be that person. Keep your promise of delivering writing worthy of a reader's time.

TOOLS, PROCESSES, AND PRACTICES

If people cannot write well, they cannot think well, and if they cannot think well, others will do their thinking for them.—George Orwell

Good writers rewrite compositions many times—each adding another layer of polish. This is not a burden because it's inherent in the writing process. It is why authors often spend years writing a book. The first draft will be a mess. And it should be. When it evolves into a manuscript where structure and content are reasonably determined—usually after several iterations—the polishing process begins. In the first draft, you, as the creator, are the audience. Once revision kicks in, your frame of reference shifts. Readers, agents, publishers, and judges become the audience.

TOOLS: A critical aspect of this polishing process is ensuring that the principles of writing—including grammar, punctuation, and word use—are followed. While not comprehensive, "Grammar Rules and Writing Principles" in the Appendix reveals principles that tend to derail rookie writers. Another tool for this is a style guide.

Style Guides: Primary sources of writing requirements are style books, the most popular being *the Elements of Style, the Chicago Manual of Style,* and *the Associated Press Stylebook.* These are referenced in "Recommended Readings" in the Appendix. Experts have varying opinions on writing rules, and this is reflected in these books. For example, one says to never use *however* to begin a sentence. Another says to never use *would* in a contraction. Pick a stylebook and apply its rules consistently. And be prepared to comply with any publisher's style preferences.

Search Engines: The most efficient tool for writing is an online search engine. If you want to learn more about anything, go online. Google is my go-to source. I access it to seek an apropos quote, to do deep research, to determine appropriate punctuation or grammar, to check spelling and the meaning and proper use of words, or whatever. Google can be a writer's best friend. The depth of information at a writer's fingertips is astounding. You can discover such uncommon details as how to spell *dagnabbit*, a word, not in dictionaries, that was introduced by farmers in the late 1800s as a substitute for swear words. (Substitutes for swear words come in handy when writing.)

PROCESSES: Two helpful processes designed to enhance the polishing effort are illustrated in the Appendix.

- Run-Through Layering Process
- Find-and-Fix Sweeps Process

Run-Throughs: When your manuscript has evolved to the point of good organization and minimal clutter—usually after three or four drafts—go over it numerous times using the run-through process, each time focusing on specific objectives that thrust the writing forward. This usually takes several months, but it is time well spent. This is revision, which is the path to authorship. If revising a draft over and over bothers you, remember *revision is writing*. It's part of the process, not the aftermath.

After each run-through, your manuscript will be improved so much that you'll be grateful you went over it one more time. For this reason, run-throughs are addictive. You'll want to do them again and again because you know that, with each pass, your composition improves.

A Layering Technique To Add Emotional Depth: Novice writers often fail to take what they write deep enough to include emotions. A three-step layering process facilitates writing deeper than mere description of facts and details.

Step 1: Write down *facts* about an incident.

Step 2: Gather *details* about those facts and elaborate.

Step 3: Explore the *feelings* people had about them.

Write with abandon about these three things. The result will be a story with interest and depth. This three-step process exposes a character's emotions, explains his behavior, and identifies what makes him the person he is. Here is how layering details and emotions onto facts enhanced my memoir:

Fact: When Dad was a boy, his older brother, whom he idolized, died. A horse had kicked his brother in the leg, and an infection developed in the wound. Penicillin had not been discovered yet, and gangrene overtook him. Years later, as a young married couple, Mom and Dad lost three babies.

50

Details: Enduring the torturous death of the young boy was traumatic for the entire family. Research on gangrene and treatments at the time revealed what the family must have experienced as this boy's leg rotted away, eventually taking his life.

The babies died in circumstances under which they likely would have been saved by medical technology today. Back then, when parents were asked how many children they had, it was not unusual to respond in terms of *surviving children.*

Feelings: These losses wounded Dad, leaving permanent emotional scars. According to his sister, he never went to church again after his brother died.

The extent to which the loss of the babies affected Dad became vividly clear when he cautioned my brother, who was playing with his toddler, "Don't get too attached to her. You could lose her." This comment is a biographical treasure, one that reveals the intensity of Dad's feelings around his personal losses and the degree to which they shaped him.

Whole chapters, rich with detail and great depth, are waiting to be derived from basic, factual information when it is taken to an emotional level. New writers often fail to do that. Thoroughly developed facts and intriguing details enhance writing, but it is emotive writing that produces splendid compositions postured to impress publishers, captivate readers, and set a writer apart.

Find-and-Fix Sweeps Process: Like the Run-Through, this is a polishing process, but it uses a computer search capability to identify common trouble spots for newbie writers. Details are presented in the Appendix.

PRACTICES: The following writing practices are designed to contribute to a writer's ability to create rich compositions that stand out from the masses.

An Idea List: Writers are thieves. Every experience is fodder for a story, essay, poem, or other writing of some sort. Most experienced writers carry something with them at all times—a phone, recorder, notepad, or whatever—in which to capture ideas for compositions. If not captured in this way, thoughts and ideas are lost the minute a writer leaves the environment in which they were created.

I transfer such information into a computerized Idea List, a forty-some page compilation of words, phrases, ideas, quotes, thoughts, similes, sayings, names, titles, and subtitles collected over time from multiple sources. This includes my ideas and those of others. (Being careful not to plagiarize, I underline words on my Idea List that are a direct quote, so I know not to use them verbatim without credit or permission.) I revamp and polish these ideas and add them to compositions, paraphrasing and putting my own spin on anything I get from anywhere other than my own head. Here are examples of jewels on my Idea List:

- A grandma's eight-year-old grandson responded to her pulling a table apart and installing leaves: "Wow! Mimi, your table is a transformer!"

- Watching a friend doing something stupid on her phone, I was fascinated by how easily she was entertained. Then, it occurred to me how entertained I was by watching her doing something stupid.

- A facelift leaves a person looking like a blowfish. A person with lip filler resembles a sock monkey. And a forehead lift creates an unnerving, perpetually surprised look. I'll not get into a butt lift, but you can imagine.

- I'm retired and wondering how soon after breakfast it's okay to take a nap.

- I'm at Cracker Barrel because gravy is a beverage.

Words and phrases on my Idea List include such treasures as: grief bacon, anti-cleavage, epitome of stupid, the medicine is mine, cushioned with foliage, so-o-o pedestrian, audacious narcissism, micro ambitious, big girl stretch pants, sit in a cloud (poet Selma Mann), wicked old, verbal dexterity, and stupid wonderful. From such notes, I harvest treasures to include in compositions. I adapted *fairy* to describe myself to my grandchildren as "the toy fairy," and I refer to "the writing fairy" in this book. Examples of layering and using an Idea List are included at the end of this chapter and in Chapter 14 on "Voice."

Mining Tidbits: Most writing is not about major life events or things of biblical proportion. Writers are not normally contemplating the world situation or the nature of the universe. Instead, they take a minor detail, a tidbit, and grow it into a story. This requires focusing on something minor and writing about it in vivid, expansive detail. An example is included at the end of this chapter. And more on tidbits is revealed in Chapter 12, "The In-Between."

Use the above tools, processes, and practices to achieve authorship and deliver the literary equivalent of a sunrise.

****

EXAMPLES FROM AN IDEA LIST

In combination, an Idea List and revision facilitate robust writing. The following jewels come from my Idea List:

- I believe my cat has a hairball in her stomach, or perhaps a sock.

- <u>If at first you don't succeed, never skydive again.</u>

- Meat is defined by vegetarians as food that has parents.

- Get a haircut. You look like a porcupine.

- Sure, I washed your Corvette. Instead of pestering me about who I am, you should be saying, "Thank you."

- I was drunk at the corner of *Walk* and *Don't Walk*.

- A grounded teen suggests, "How about if I go to the party, but I don't have fun?"

- His idea of enjoying the outdoors is being drunk in a gazebo.

- His education included quantum physics, but he couldn't help his child with third-grade math.

- I'm sorry I'm late to the meeting. I didn't want to be here.

- As a parent, if you think things are going well, you obviously don't have a clue what is going on.

- Nothing will make you crazier than trying to figure out a crazy person.

For weighty essays, I mine more serious, Idea List gems:

- Just because you think something in your head doesn't make it true. It is a thought.

- Political views are not facts. Opinions are not facts. Facts are facts.

- People tend to accept that which supports what they already believe and reject information that supports what they don't want to believe. Reality and rational thought have little to do with opinions.

- Otherwise reasonable people will believe anything if you provide a fix for their "ruin."

- Increments of time are gifts from the universe. Every day you are gifted a new start.

- Initially, aging stalked me. Then, it crept up and grabbed me by the soul with the fervor of a lion downing its prey.

- Nature makes no promises, but at its core, it is the result of natural laws and is, therefore, predictable —except when it's not.

- People are savages on the Internet.

- Listening doesn't just happen. You must do it.

- When you are working, time is your enemy. After you retire, time is gentle. It is your friend.

- If you live long enough, you will eventually become cute again.

- Forgiveness snuck in. The ravaged heart healed. And the pain went away, almost unnoticed.

TURNING A TIDBIT INTO A STORY

Writers Are Thieves
by Nikki Hanna

At a writers conference in New York City, I took a break from an all-night writing marathon. An Oklahoma woman out of my element, I sat in a diner at two o'clock in the morning, drinking coffee. The Friday night crowd trailed in after a frenzied night of fun. Some patrons were decked out in nightclub garb. In contrast, I looked like a French café slouch in clothes comfortable enough to be classified as pajamas and hair resembling a cat toy. I was not bothered by my appearance, though. In New York City, nothing is peculiar.

One might wonder why a sixty-something-year-old woman from Tulsa, Oklahoma, graced this setting. I was a writer, and serious writers, at one time or another, make a pilgrimage of sorts to New York City. A quest for coffee created a bonus adventure for this tourist who stumbled upon a flavor of the city's night life. Writers are thieves, and I decided to observe the action for the purpose of stealing ideas for a future composition. Prospects were abundant.

Exposed young girls, with vocabularies embellished with the words *like* and *whatever*, and blustery, cocky young men, with shaved heads or dreads and baggy pants slung low enough to reveal underwear, coexisted splendidly after a Friday night of partying. The women paraded by— wobbling in four-inch heels—as young men in the next booth delivered a testosterone-fueled pick-up line, "Oh, my god! You are so beautiful. Oh, my god!" They didn't say this to me, of course. I was still trying to lose baby fat from my firstborn child forty-eight years ago.

These comments were directed at rumpled, smudged-up, glassy-eyed unfortunates in hemlines so short it appeared they had put on blouses and forgotten their skirts. One girl's dress was hiked up so high that the crotch of her thong was visible in front, and her bare ass in back. Although this visual was an assault on my mind (I thought, *Gawd*), the guys were so taken by *thong girl* that they pounded the table. Unable to contain themselves, they rose from their seats as if their butts were filled with helium. Following her, they omitted the "You are so beautiful," and said, "Oh, my god! Oh, my god! Oh, my god!"

A few gang-like fellows were so rambunctious I expected someone would throw them out, but no one paid attention. So after contemplating whether a bullet could penetrate the wall of my booth, I abandoned the concerned tourist role and settled in for a session of discreet observation, while making a mental note: *The next time I come to New York City, I will explore the prospect of a more sophisticated hotel, one that leaves chocolates on my pillow and whose guests drink Grand Marnier at two in the morning.*

I hung around longer than intended because my waiter, *the swiper*, periodically passed by at the speed of light, swooping up my half-filled coffee cup for refills. Since I'd dosed it with the required daily supplement of fiber, I had to drink each successive cup to ensure I got my thirty grams. Once accomplished, I left with a severe caffeine buzz, but not before overhearing a confounding conversation in the next booth.

A dazed young woman wore Christmas lights as a necklace, and her head occasionally dangled perilously close to her catsup-covered french fries. She lamented to her male companions that her boyfriend would be furious with her for getting so-o-o wasted. One of the noble fellows comforted her, "It'll be all right. He'll get over it." To prove his point, he said, "I threw up on my girlfriend once, and she's still my girlfriend."

57

You know you are in the writing zone when hours later your coffee is cold and your breakfast is still on a plate next to your computer.

Chapter 4

WRITING PRINCIPLES

Adverbs are not your friends. The road to hell is paved with them. They are like dandelions—one is pretty, but they can take over your writing.—Stephen King

When judging writing contests, I get a flavor of what an agent must go through when evaluating manuscripts. Submissions usually represent a normal Bell Curve, with about twenty percent at the top and at the bottom and the rest somewhere in the middle. All but the top few entries will be "out of the running" immediately. Competition is fierce. Solid craftsmanship is required to have any chance at getting into the top group. Principles of writing craft are what set a writer apart. Following are crucial ones.

SHOW, DON'T TELL

Don't tell me the moon is shining; show me the glint of light on broken glass.—Anton Chekhov

Telling is not wrong, but it's best to show when possible. The following words suggest a writer is telling: *feel, felt, knew, seemed, noticed, looked, saw, heard, learned, realized, wondered, guessed, hoped,* or *thought.*

To show, rather than tell, use dialogue, behavior, expressions, or actions. This means that rather than saying a character is weird, show he is weird. Make him weird through what he says and does, what others say about him, or what happens to him because of his weird behavior. But know also that sometimes you just gotta *tell* through narrative or exposition (a big word for telling).

Occasionally, writers get carried away with showing, while the reader is hankering to simply and efficiently be given information. Don't be afraid to tell. Still, showing is a magical opportunity for a writer to communicate.

Screenwriters develop a knack for *show, don't tell* because they are limited to telling stories through vision and sound as opposed to through narration. Examples of *show, don't tell* are presented at the end of this chapter.

ACTIVE VERSUS PASSIVE VOICE

Write strong. Enough said.

To write strong, writers are advised to use active voice. It is stronger and more efficient than passive voice (it requires fewer words). However, passive voice is not technically wrong, and it comes in handy for making a sentence work or for varying sentence structure. Just don't overuse it. In general, it's best if the flavor of writing is strong.

With active voice, the subject does the action. In passive voice, the object of the verb does the action. Note the presence of passive verbs in the following passive sentences and how they contrast with the stronger verbs in the active sentences. In the active statements, the person performing the action is at the beginning of the sentence.

Passive: The wedding dress *was ironed* by Mattie.
Active: Mattie *ironed* the wedding dress.

Passive: Mashed potatoes *were eaten* by Tony.
Active: Tony *ate* mashed potatoes.

Passive: The runway *will be graced* by models.
Active: Models *will grace* the runway.

Passive: That style *is being* worn by everyone.
Active: Everyone *wears* that style.

Eliminate as many passive sentences as you can. If the prospect of finding them through grammatical analysis makes your head hurt, lighten up. Identifying passive voice is easy. The verb determines if a sentence is active or passive. Do a computerized search (using the Find command) on *be, being,* and *been.* These words almost always signal passive voice. *Was, were, are* and *is* may also do so. (Not all sentences using these verbs are passive.) Replace these weak verbs with those with more muscle. Research *active voice* online. Use it, and your writing will be more potent.

OPTIMAL WORD USE

The longer, more clever, more impressive, or more dazzling word is often not the right one. And a word that draws attention to the writing is the wrong word.

Probably nothing is more important to writing strong than writing efficiently. This requires that writers eliminate unnecessary words, select the right words, and use effective syntax (arrangement of words and phrases).

Words that are common candidates for possible deletion are listed in the Appendix under the "Find-and-Fix Sweeps Process." These words are not necessarily wrong. Most are in every book or composition, including this one. Many of them are even essential, but they are also often overused, unnecessary, or banal. Some are out of favor with writing experts, agents, and publishers because they cry out for a better word or no word. Search for them, take them out, or rewrite where you deem appropriate.

In addition to eliminating excess words, selecting the right words is crucial. The right word in the right place can make all the difference. When polishing a composition, look for opportunities to find better—more unique, colorful, and descriptive—words, ones that perfectly describe the situation or communicate your intended meaning. When a word produces a visual or elicits an emotional response, it is magical.

While doing a run-through, the word *important* caught my attention. It was an okay word, but a common one, and it seemed too ordinary to express the intended message. With a thesaurus, I discovered several more descriptive words that were a better fit, such as pivotal, paramount, essential, crucial, notable, and fundamental. I chose *notable*, a distinguished word that jazzed up the sentence and was more descriptive of the situation than *important.*

In her book, *Reading Like a Writer,* Francine Prose said to put every word on trial. If you don't go through your document looking for words to take out or to replace with better words, you are missing an opportunity to stand out as a writer. Don't overdo, though. You don't want to be known as a showboat or a gonzo writer.

The propensity to overdo is what causes some experts to discourage use of a thesaurus. Stephen King is somewhat anti-thesaurus. He said, "Any word you have to hunt for in a thesaurus is the wrong word." I don't agree. I am pro-thesaurus. Just make certain you don't look for a big word, a fancy one, a complicated one, or one that shows off your intellect. Look for the right word —one that gets your message across efficiently and, in some cases, in a colorful manner. Use words that sing, zing, paint a picture, and keep the reader awake while communicating just the right meaning.

It's important to note that big words are not necessarily bad. Wrong words are bad, and big words are often wrong words in the wrong places, like a Randy Newman song at a wedding. A minor distinction can make a huge difference. Mark Twain said, "The difference between the right word and the almost right word is the difference between lightning and a lightning bug."

Angela Ackerman and Becca Puglisi have a series of thesauruses that list word alternatives, including: *The Emotion Thesaurus, The Character Expression Thesaurus, The Negative Trait Thesaurus, The Positive Trait Thesaurus,* and *The Rural Setting Thesaurus.* Barbara J. McMinn has two thesauruses of phrases. And—get this—I ran across a thesaurus for romance writers. Unfortunately, I was so distracted by the erotic content when I perused it that I failed to take note of the name of the author or her book. Sorry.

BE DIRECT: William Zinsser said, "Don't say you were a bit confused, or sort of tired, or a little depressed, or somewhat annoyed. Be confused. Be tired. Be depressed. Be annoyed. Don't hedge your prose with timidities. Good writing is lean and confident." Well said. Also, don't say, "She stated to cry" or "She began to cry." Say, "She cried."

CULTURAL REFERENCES: Word choice is influenced by the environment in which the story is being told. While editing, look for the appropriateness of cultural references. For example, if you are writing a Western and need an animal, it makes no sense to use a zebra. Similarly, if the setting is Africa, a bull, buffalo, or coyote is not a good fit. This sounds simple enough, but you would be surprised how often a word in a story is incongruent with the time, culture, or location.

SETTING DESCRIPTIONS

Readers need a sense of time, place, and surroundings.

Describing settings is a splendid creative experience— an opportunity to embellish a scene. Readers crave a backdrop to a story in both fiction and nonfiction. Few writers do this well. If you do so, you will stand out.

A run-through of your composition, focused entirely on opportunities to use expressive descriptions, will enhance your story and add flare and style. Finesse is required when doing this. It's imperative that setting descriptions do not distract from a story or interrupt its pace. Expertly place such details throughout the piece.

A brilliant writer described potted plants on both sides of an entrance as "earrings." That setting description was so compelling that, to this day, when I see twin pots on doorsteps or porches, I think of them as earrings. This description also hints at who lives in the house—a woman (most guys don't water plants) with a strong pride of ownership and nurturing tendencies. I've been unable to identify this author, so I cannot give her credit here; however, I'm compelled to convey her description because it is genius.

This example shows how a setting description can define a character through implication. How a person gravitates to an environment or creates one says a lot about him. Mary Buckham's book, *Writing Active Setting,* shows how to master communicating a culture, an environment, or even a character's personality through setting details. Such information has the potential to make all the difference in a story.

POINT OF VIEW

Because both rookie and seasoned writers struggle with point-of-view technique, mastering it is an opportunity to stand out.

Every story or scene is written from someone's point of view (POV), which represents from whose perspective the story is told. Within the first few sentences of a book, chapter, or scene, readers need to know who that person is —a character, a narrator, or even the author. Identify the POV in the first few sentences of each scene or chapter, and have only one. Describe the environment, characters, and story action from that POV character's perspective.

Use the POV person's name the first time they are mentioned, and then use a third-person personal pronoun (he or she) for them in the rest of the chapter or scene (unless the name is needed for clarification). No other character should be identified as *he* or *she.* (Use their names.) POV technique is complicated but crucial to writing well. Do an online search and study up.

The Nick Carraway character in *The Great Gatsby* is an example of a first-person narrator. The story is told from his point of view. Readers don't get into the heads of Gatsby,

Daisy, Tom, or anyone else. Fitzgerald tells their stories through their connections with Nick.

The POV is typically that of the main character or a narrator, but it can change for strategic reasons, usually at scene or chapter breaks. Execute such shifts so as not to jolt or confuse readers. Newbie writers are often unaware of the point of view from which they write. They dart all over the place, head-hopping away (switching POV characters without cluing-in the reader). Make no willy-nilly shifts. And let the reader know when a point of view changes.

SIMILES AND METAPHORS

Introduce a simile or a metaphorical concept only occasionally, and make it incredibly clever. Otherwise, you risk looking like an amateur.

Similes and metaphors are figures of speech that describe an object or action in a way that isn't literally true but is illustrated by making a comparison:

Simile: Compares two things directly by using *like, as, as though,* or *similar to.* Examples: *fierce like Santa Ana winds, as indifferent as cattle, lit up like an all-night casino,* and *incongruent like a nose ring and bifocals.* Be careful. Overdoing similes reduces their effect and can appear amateurish.

Metaphor: Compares two things that aren't alike but have something in common. It refers to one thing by mentioning another. Examples: *He's a couch potato. That wrestler is an animal. The classroom was a zoo,* or *a beehive of activity.*

Metaphors go beyond the literal and may be used in a broader sense without such an obvious statement as those above. For example, in Fitzgerald's *The Great Gatsby*, a billboard with eye glasses on it was a metaphor for someone watching the incident that occurred under it.

A metaphor can be silly. Comparing a salad to the diversity of a police force, with the laws as dressing and the croutons representing the SWAT team, is not going to work, unless humor is your goal. ("Examples of Similes and Metaphors" are included at the end of this chapter.)

TENSION AND CONFLICT

Tension comes from a nagging itch to the reader that something is not right.—William Bernhardt

Tension in the form of either a macro or micro conflict in every scene is what keeps readers reading. Tension evolves from uncomfortable situations. People with conflicting goals and perspectives make others anxious, and that is what tension is about. A clever writer makes his audience worry. I worried my heart out when I read *Lonesome Dove* because the author made me care about the characters. That's why I read it a second time.

Conflict is seductive. It is expressed through narrative, dialogue, and action and comes from characters' internal responses to external stimulation. Friction between protagonists and antagonists is what plot is all about, but don't limit it to those characters. Use discord generously, but for the most part, limit it to one incident per scene. The intensity of a story needs to ebb and flow. Tension from back-to-back contention or excessively long episodes of dissent can wear out a reader.

ELICITING READER EMOTIONS

Make the reader laugh or cry or shiver. Make him wonder, give him a lesson learned, or all of these.

Tapping into the emotions of characters makes a reader feel on a visceral level. If you can't make him feel, you won't be able to hold him. Doing so requires frequent references to the five senses. Touch is powerful, but it is often ignored by writers, except in the romance genre. So is smell, which is particularly potent. Someone said, "Smell never lies." (How many veterans have you heard describe Vietnam by its smell?) People listen to music for the emotional effects, eat dessert for the sweet buzz, and search out sunsets for their visual impact. And then there is the gleeful anticipation or gripping angst of the sixth sense—intuition.

Introduce emotions and sensory responses into your writing. Without them, characters fall flat and do not come alive for the reader. Some experts recommend including a sensory response of some sort on every page. In fiction, be generous with sensory responses to conflict and tension. And don't be afraid to include emotional details in nonfiction as well, especially in memoir, inspirational writing, and personal essays.

Become an expert at describing emotive responses. That's what wins contests, attracts publishers, and creates fans.

USING QUOTES

Someone else's words enhance your own, add interest, and strengthen your message.

Quotes are most often used in nonfiction. To find a quote, search online by typing *quotes/name/subject* (e.g., quotes/williamzinsser/voice) in the search bar. My favorite quote sources for humor are Erma Bombeck, George Carlin, and Steve Martin; the movies *Tombstone, Steel Magnolias*, and *The Big Chill*; and the Internet site *coolfunnyquotes.com*. For writing craft, my favorite quote sources are: Stephen King, William Zinsser, William Bernhardt, Anne Lamott, and Amanda Patterson (BrainyQuote). For wisdom, my go-to source is Winnie the Pooh. Really. A lucrative general quote site is *quotesandsayings.com*.

When you quote someone, limit the quote to two or three sentences and give credit to the author. If more than that is used, ask permission. You will likely get it. Writers like to be quoted. It's good marketing.

CIVIL LEGAL ISSUES: It's important to avoid plagiarism —using other people's words without their consent. Most writers who violate this rule don't do it on purpose. It's easy to accidentally do so because writers often don't know the source of information in their heads or in notes. The important thing is that you don't purposely use another writer's words and portray them as your own. Paraphrasing provides a way to share information without a direct quote, but even then, attribute the information to the original source.

Another legal threat for writers is defamation. Nonfiction writers are more susceptible to this pitfall because they write about real people and events, as opposed to a fantasy world.

Dead people can't sue, but their families might. Even if you have not plagiarized or defamed anyone, you can still be sued, in which case you must defend your position. The following approaches help limit risk:

Don't fudge facts. Untrue facts that have a negative effect on a person are considered defamatory. The "truth" is a defense, but truth is defined differently by everyone and is often hard to prove.

Get written permission. This is your best protection when quoting something written, if it is more than three sentences. Writings before 1923 are considered public domain and are not copyrighted.

I had been advised to get permission to write about anyone in my memoir. I didn't do it. My four brothers would have used that as proof their sister was obsessive. So I tried not to embarrass anyone and let some people read parts about themselves in advance. Ten years later, no one has objected to anything. I suspect many memoirists take the same risk.

Write gently about people. Avoid revenge writing, and don't call Aunt Maude bat-shit crazy. Call her zany. Make her funny, and let her read what you wrote before you use it. Difficult people are often proud of their contrary dispositions. If written about with good humor, the person may love what you wrote and become your champion.

Litigation outcomes are unpredictable. Avoidance of issues is the best bet. Calvin Coolidge said, "I have never been hurt by what I have not said." Consult a legal expert if you have concerns.

THE EDGE: Because so many writers don't understand craft or don't embrace it, doing so gives the writer who does a substantial edge. *Show, don't tell* is an effective tool for creating "edge." The examples below demonstrate how *showing* run-throughs improved first drafts.

****

EXAMPLES OF *SHOW, DON'T TELL*

Tell: She stood in the pediatric care unit, staring at the baby and worrying about his future. A nurse entered and took his blood.

Show: As she stood in the pediatric care unit, tears welled up in her eyes. She wiped them on her sleeve. *Be strong, Grandma, be strong. You can do this.* A nurse entered. Soon, the baby wailed as needles jabbed at his tiny body.

Tell: She wasn't the outdoorsy type, but she had a strong attraction to country boys. If one brought home a buck, she was up for rewarding her hunter with breakfast.

Show: Although not the outdoorsy type with a propensity to lean up against a tree in a picture, for her, country boys had an undeniable appeal. As she pulled into the driveway, she noticed a skinned and gutted deer hanging from a tree in the front yard, dripping blood. Hounds jumped up trying to get a piece of it. She scurried inside to cook her exhausted hunter biscuits and gravy before putting the groceries away.

Tell: The club's music and lights created an atmosphere that fueled Dawn's excitement for the dance.

Show: A high feasted on Dawn's psyche as she entered the dance hall. Music pounded, and whiskey-colored lights shone mystically through a haze of smoke. Shadowy figures lingered throughout. Her anticipation matched the energy of the atmosphere, and she became at one with the place.

Tell: Devon was smitten with Madelyn, which changed everything. He cleaned up his act and did what he could to appeal to her, including working out and getting a tan.

Show: After meeting Madelyn, Devon displayed the exuberance of a hyped-up Yorkie. He worked out; cut his hair; trimmed his mountain-man beard; shopped at Abercrombie; and traded hotdogs, Cheetos, and Oreos for chicken soup and fruit. With his newfound tan, he could have been mistaken for a Middle Eastern terrorist.

Tell: Travis was the redneck type with a passion for guns and four-wheel-drive, diesel trucks. Although Belle suspected he loved his dog, horse, and turkey more than her, she was sure he had feelings for her.

Show: Travis had a sign on his front door with a picture of a gun on it that read, "I don't call 911." His bipolar dog, Brute, was so mean and unpredictable that, when Travis didn't answer his phone, Belle worried Brute had eaten him. Although Travis was unsuccessful at stopping his turkey from attacking her when she got out of her car, she was convinced Travis loved her because he let her drive his truck to town for beer.

Tell: Conner knew Brook was hurting inside. He felt sorry for her.

Show: Conner cupped Brook's hands in his and said, "I'm sorry. What can I do?"

EXAMPLES OF SIMILES AND METAPHORS

SIMILE: A figure of speech that compares two things directly, using *like, as*, *as though*, or *similar to*.

- The lady was classy, *like* Beluga caviar.

- The site offered as many options *as* a casino buffet.

- Your texts are *like* teases from the universe.

- His meth habit caused him to tweak *like* a skating rink strobe light.

- A savage, purple-tinged hairdo, *similar to* sofa stuffing, gave away her age and condition.

- Orange dreadlocks made it appear *as though* Cheetos were sticking out of his head.

- It was *as though* a soft, well-worn flannel shirt had brushed the skin lightly, soothed the soul, and cradled the spirit.

METAPHOR: A figure of speech that compares two unlike things that have something in common. It refers to one thing by mentioning another.

- The fix was just a band-aid.

- He is a walking dictionary.

- Her eyes were ice cold.

- The peaceful water, a mirror reflecting trees and mountains, grounded the scene.

Everyone knows you can't trust spell check or autocorrect. If you text, "I'll call you when I leave the hotel," and autocorrect changes it to, "I'll sex you when I leave the hotel," don't be surprised if the response is "Hot damn!"

Chapter 5

CHARACTER DEVELOPMENT

The character that lasts is an ordinary guy with some extraordinary qualities.—Raymond Chandler

In his book, *On Writing,* Stephen King, a master of character development, talks about how to create characters and to surprise readers with their actions. He says, "I try to create sympathy for my characters, then turn the monsters loose."

William Bernhardt, in his book, *Creating Character,* suggests that it's okay for people in fiction to seem larger than life. Since characters are not real, they can be painted in outlandish ways. He says, "Create characters who are so extraordinary that they will do what a normal person would not and act when an average person would not."

Make every character, no matter how minor, interesting—no cardboard characters or stereotypes. When developing a character, convey to the reader where his limits are. That says a lot about a person. Everyone has a line they won't cross. Have your hero face that line. And when he crosses it and does a bad thing, have it be for an important reason, perhaps to protect someone.

CHARACTER DESCRIPTION TECHNIQUES

Portray characters from physical, mental, visual, and behavioral perspectives and make certain they change over time.

Heroes should have flaws; and villains, redeeming qualities. When describing characters, *show, don't tell* as much as possible. Let actions, behaviors, interactions, and dialogue reflect personal attributes and reveal what is going on in people's heads. Below, are qualities to consider when describing a character:

External qualities: appearance, style, clothes, hair, eyes, skin, teeth, expressions, gait, weight, height, build, posture, movement, skills

Internal qualities: witty, ambitious, friendly, staid, adventurous, mean, quirky, anxious, meek, naive, criminal, fun, carefree, aggressive, generous

The character's world: home, vehicle, pet, lawn, recliner, diet, workplace, wardrobe, car, hobbies, associations, location, what's in the refrigerator

To make a character endearing, assign him some kind of misfortune he doesn't deserve, and have him be exceptionally good at something. Give him a sidekick or another important character who likes him, even with his faults, and who says so. A perfect example of this is the eccentric character in the television series *Monk*. He was not a typical leading character, but rather, an ordinary guy with extraordinary qualities and a loyal supporter.

A writer can use characters to make a story stand out. Go through your manuscript and enhance it to present people with depth who act in appealing and intriguing ways so readers connect and care about them. Make them likable, though imperfect. This will make them come alive for the reader. When writing nonfiction, look for these qualities in real people. Consider these attributes:

Portray characters as:
- Complex
- Vulnerable
- Burdened with grievances
- Tortured by unfortunate experiences
- Desperate and driven
- Conflicted
- Evolving

Give characters these qualities:
- Special abilities and exceptional qualities
- Unusual traits
- An obsession or a passion
- A purpose or a disturbing void
- A temperament
- Strengths, weaknesses, and flaws
- Hopes and regrets
- Losses
- Backstory
- A pet
- Relationships—positive and negative

Where possible, reveal a person's characteristics without explicitly stating them. Use behavior, dialogue, and enough visual detail and action to convey the essence of a person—their "way of being" in the world. The following paragraph gets into the head of a detective who was ravaged by a connection years ago that haunted her still. Notice that her emotional state and her past are implied through the story rather than directly stated:

> As Piper sat in her parked car, the couple she was tailing exited the restaurant. The man held the woman's hand as he assisted her down the curb and, with his hand on her back, led her through the parking lot to the car. Piper, still single after divorcing her husband twenty-some years ago, observed the man open the car door for the woman. Piper searched for a word to describe their connection and came up with "cherished." *I've never felt that. Now, I'm not sure I want to.* She prepared to follow the couple with thoughts of Deacon creeping into her head.

Sprinkle character descriptions throughout a story, rather than bunching them up into expository dumps. The above paragraph reveals internal conflict and creates curiosity by alluding to Piper's backstory (history). This is accomplished through thoughts and innuendo rather than by telling that history. If another character were present, the same thing could have been accomplished through dialogue. Note that curiosity was created through implication by the mere mention of Deacon's name. Here are more tips:

- Make character descriptions deep but succinct.

- Describe a character through his world as he travels through it: home, vehicle, pets, workplace, associations, activities, hobbies, music, sofa, diet.

- Show a character's energy level. That says a lot.

- Describe physical characteristics in colorful ways, rather than literally. For example, describe a person with big ears as having "ears that stick out like suicide car doors."

- Use dialogue to describe a person's life. A woman sitting on a park bench, watching children play, reveals the hassles of motherhood as she asks her companions, "Why are my clothes always wet?"

- How a person moves expresses their essence. A writer, whom I've not been able to identify, portrayed Alec Baldwin in a clever way by describing his gait: "He has the unbending, straight-armed gait of someone trying to prevent clothes from rubbing against sunburned skin."

Introduce characters with enough—but not too much—visual detail and behavior to reveal their intrinsic nature. Consider what this description I wrote implies about a guy named Tank: "He cleaned his spartan, beige house with a leaf blower once a year whether it needed it or not, leaving an odor of gasoline that lingered for weeks."

Here is something else I wrote that introduces a woman of character:

> She wears black but glows in contrast to its darkness. She is intuitive and level-headed. She boldly speaks her mind with splendid candor and attitude. She leaves her mark wherever she goes and touches the souls of the troubled. She is both a savage warrior

and a tender lover of peace of mind. She is remarkable in the way only the powerful can be. She is woman. They call her Dakota.

This description breaks several writing rules:

- The length is a tad too long.

- Several adjectives and adverbs are used.

- The description *tells* rather than *shows*.

- It is generally not good to start every sentence with the same word. (To be effective, this technique needs to be blatantly done so the intent of the repetition is obvious.)

Stylistically, though, these departures from general craft requirements work here because they efficiently portray the character. The reader concludes that Dakota is a person worthy of their concern and admiration as well as someone to be reckoned with. Following this description of Dakota with details of an emotional connection between her and another person or animal, could further advance her image.

CHARACTER PROFILES: Making readers care about characters requires creating intriguing and emotionally vulnerable ones. Before starting a story, list the qualities of your main characters from physical, mental, and behavioral perspectives—taking care to distinguish them from one another. Give each one a past that influences the present. Share this information gradually over the course of the story—not all at once in a descriptive tirade. Make characters' behaviors consistent with their profiles, but include occasional deviations that surprise readers.

Main characters should be three-dimensional, which means they have a past, present, and future. Add this information to their profiles.

A dash of panache when describing a character delights readers who crave the dramatic or the unusual. Make characters complex, as I did in this case:

> Roger was an "outlier," a delightfully unique person who was a challenge to rein in. He ran in a higher gear than most, and his impetuous nature drove him to jump on beds in furniture stores and to consider mooning an appropriate activity, even at the seasoned age of fifty-two. His intelligence and professional persona effectively masked aberrant behavioral tendencies to all except those who knew him well.

Later, I described him further:

> Roger had the softest, shiniest blue eyes Mandy had ever seen, and she believed he had a good heart. He was the only man to ask her what kind of music she wanted to hear when she got into his car. Until she met him, she had listened to her share of Boston, ZZ Top, The Dead, Leon Russell and, worst of all, ranting and raving talk radio hosts. Roger delivered the slow jazz, soft rock, or classic country she loved. This did not, however, mitigate her suspicion that his accommodating behavior was an act of seduction. In spite of this awareness, she chose to ignore that prospect.

This complicated character description creates curiosity and suggests conflict, tension, and drama to come.

THE MAGIC OF ANCILLARY CHARACTERS

Supporting characters have the potential to embellish a story like gems in a necklace. And minor characters can glow like Fourth-of-July sparklers.

Ancillary characters fall into two categories—supporting and minor. Either can make all the difference in a story. Masterfully developing them makes a writer more competitive because so many writers fail to capitalize on them. These key players offer lucrative opportunities to enhance a narrative. Consider Chewbacca in *Star Wars,* Doc Holliday in *Tombstone,* Ouiser (pronounced Weezer) in *Steel Magnolias,* and Chester in *Gunsmoke.*

SUPPORTING CHARACTERS: The emotional connection between a supporting character and a major one is fundamental. Reflect on the coupling of characters in sitcoms and movies. There is almost always an engaging oddball connected, in some way, to the main character or villain. A zany sidekick provides a superb foil for a protagonist. Also, a comical henchman coupled with a villain provides opportunities to add spice to a story and to soften the blows of dastardly antics.

Animals make effective vehicles for showing attachments and for introducing humor. Who hasn't cried over *Marley* and *Bambi* or laughed over Tom Hanks and the slobbering hound, Hooch. Even "things" can inspire affection. Consider the robot characters in *Star Wars,* who endeared themselves to children and adults and delivered unexpected humor in the midst of serious crises. By giving such players a greater presence, a writer can shape and enhance a story. Supporting characters can:

- Inform readers of story details.

- Move the story forward.

- Create anticipation and curiosity.

- Add humor and entertainment.

- Build tension and conflict.

- Introduce drama.

- Exhibit captivating human dynamics.

- Evoke emotional responses in readers.

- Give main characters someone to talk to. (Dialogue reveals thoughts, temperaments, and histories.)

I came across an old *Gunsmoke* show and, having just studied character roles in a workshop, I saw Chester's role in a new light. Development of his unique personality, vocal quirks, dress, and physical attributes (including a limp) provided comedic elements in a subtle but effective way. His purpose, though, was not limited to comic effect or sidekick support, as I had originally thought. The observations and information he shared through dialogue provided the viewer with details vital to advancing the story.

MINOR CHARACTERS: Supporting characters usually have a more important role than minor ones, and they stay in the story longer. Minor players are fleeting, entering the story just long enough to serve their purposes. They may or may not have names. If you do give a minor character a name, make it fit his personality, his generation, and the genre in which you're writing. Sprinkle minor players throughout a book. Don't miss opportunities to make them colorful. Create no ordinary characters. Even the following nameless old man, who was only briefly in a short story I wrote, was painted as a colorful guy:

> After he front-ended the car, the stooped old geezer with a Civil War general's beard and pant legs tucked inside well-worn boots, exited his clunker to survey the damage. Feathers dangled from the back of his crumpled alligator hat.
>
> He walked like a scruffy hillbilly moseying out to his front porch to lounge on a rocker and gander at the sunset while communing with coon dogs and waiting for supper.
>
> When a policeman arrived, the fellow lumbered up to him and explained, "I drived down heres from Alabama to gets a tattoo, and my shirt was a itchin' it, so I's lookin' for a T-shirt place. Then, dagnabbit, dis happened. I's paid $200 for dat thar car."
>
> The policeman responded, without looking up, as he wrote a ticket, "It's worth about twenty bucks now."

Even the policeman had flair, though he had no name. If the old fellow had a name, it would have been something like Mooney or Rooster.

Use supporting and temporary minor characters to add flavor to your story. Make them comedic, colorful, or quaint. Not doing so is a missed opportunity. Details on creating comedic characters are included in Chapter 16 on "Humor."

****

EXAMPLE OF A KEY MINOR CHARACTER

Minor characters are often hard-working key players. A hotel registration clerk sets up a story I wrote about older ladies naively checking into a hotel on a beach in Florida during spring break. He foreshadows events, hints at theme, and differentiates the three main characters through observation.

Jason, the youthful hotel registration clerk, shifted nervously from foot to foot as he observed three older ladies approach. They pulled along suitcases almost as big as they were and juggled citrus-colored sun hats, large purses, designer sunglasses, and souvenir bags from airport shops. These were, no doubt, well-travelled women accustomed to exclusive hotels that offer bellmen, chocolates on pillows at night, and safes in which to store jewelry. Jason possessed a rare appreciation for such women. They reminded him of his grandmother, whom he considered a frigging supernova. He greeted them with a genuine smile.

DeeDee asked, "What's your name, young man?"

"Jason."

"Well, Jason, these gals, Roxie and Brook, are in a foul mood, so let's you and I talk. How about an upgraded room?"

"Let's do it." He hustled to check them in. *The lobby's rare interlude of calm could change at any moment.* "I'm putting you in an end unit on the top floor."

"Nice," DeeDee responded.

To Jason's surprise, Roxie performed a celebratory hop completely out of character for an older woman and put her hand up to Brook for a high five. They missed each other's hands and tried unsuccessfully several more times to connect before transitioning into playful hitting. *Well, that's novel. I hope the old gals don't hurt themselves.*

Roxie continued badgering Brook about her ex. "What kind of idiot is a fan of Sharknado? The man's a dolt."

Brook's body stiffened. "Shut up."

"You shut up."

"No, you shut up."

"You S-H-U-T U-P."

"You both shut up," DeeDee interjected.

"Are you sisters?" Jason asked.

"No," DeeDee said. "I don't know these people, and they are bothering me."

Roxie smiled mockingly at DeeDee.

Brook brushed wild auburn curls from her forehead as she dug in her purse and pulled out a tissue, "He did suck the life out of me. So why am I hurting?"

"Because you're an idiot," Roxie responded.

"Why would you say such an awful thing?"

"I'm trying to be poetic."

Jason forced himself to focus as he put iridescent rubber security bands on the ladies' wrists. *This should distract them from the man-rage.*

"Arm candy," said Roxie. "Makes me feel sporty." She struck a series of ridiculous Hans and Franz poses.

DeeDee shook her head.

Jason laughed. *Maybe their sense of humor will carry them through their stay.* "You're checked in. Would you like tickets for a free breakfast buffet?"

"Oh, yes," DeeDee responded.

"How about coupons for drinks at the beach tiki bar?"

"Fabulous."

"Perhaps you'd like earplugs?"

A puzzled expression crossed DeeDee's face, but she shrugged and responded, "How nice."

"Have a nice stay. Let me know if you need anything." Jason said. He shook his head as he watched the ladies walk away, wrestling luggage, and all talking at the same time. A security guard stopped them and examined their wrist bands. *Hell is just around the corner.*

* * *

As the ladies turned the corner to the elevators, sand grated on the their designer sandals. A restless, festive crowd of teens in skimpy swimsuits clustered around the elevator doors. Two cops escorted cuffed, desolate-looking juveniles through the crowd. Abrasive noises and bump and grind music blasted in from the beach. When an elevator door opened, screams and laughter exploded into the hallway as boisterous teens poured out.

Going shoulder-to-shoulder with the feral children, Roxie pushed her way onto the elevator and cleared a way for her friends. "How much Ambien did you bring?" she asked DeeDee, who was squashed into the corner.

"Not enough," she responded.

An oiled-up, tatted teen in a skimpy bikini asked the ladies, "What college are you from?"

Good dialogue is efficient. As Anne Lamott said, "No" is a complete sentence.

Chapter 6

USE OF DIALOGUE

Dialogue is the wizard of writing. It brings readers and characters closer together.

Dialogue is a literary technique in which two or more people are engaged in conversation. It is used to tell a story; to reveal vital details; to convey mood, theme, and backstory; and to expose what's going on in a character's head. It also breaks up too-long commentary, introduces humor, explains behavior, and conveys emotion in a way nothing else can. Dialogue flushes out characters, paints pictures of them, and describes them through pronunciation and diction. It sets the tone, energizes the story at pivotal times, and moves the storyline along.

Dialogue works hard. It is efficient. Its effectiveness is illustrated in this comment a wife made to a confidante: "I hate NASCAR . . . and Bruce Willis." This economical statement defined her husband, herself, and their relationship.

The following comments of a prickly old fellow with a cantankerous disposition reveal his nature vividly through his own words rather than through description:

Wilber bombarded his niece, Madelyn, with a substantial dose of complaints on her visit, causing her to suspect he possessed a gray aura. Nestled in a well-worn, oversized recliner capable of throwing him out with the push of a button, he said, "I don't like nobody." The crotchety old codger delivered his next reflection in his long menu of complaints, "And I don't like dogs." This was in spite of a tiny one nestled contentedly in his lap.

Madelyn expected him to tell her he hated babies or teddy bears next. So she introduced a more positive topic. But Wilber hijacked the trend with a testy comment about the weather before moving on to this: "And I don't like morning people . . . or mornings . . . or people."

"How are you feeling these days, Wilber?"

"I feel like I'm in a dryer being tumbled. And most of my friends are dead."

Madelyn said, "I'm sorry." When she departed, she said, "Have a nice day, Wilber."

He responded, "I have other plans."

This example shows the power of characters speaking. Serious writers learn how to tap into that power.

EFFECTIVE DIALOGUE

Make certain all dialogue is relevant. Have people speak because they want something.

In an interview, Alan Watt, author of *The 90-Day Rewrite,* said, "A single line can reveal a great deal about a character." He used the following scenario to illustrate this point:

I ran into a friend whom I hadn't seen in a while. "How's life?" I asked.

He sighed. "I want a car with a door that opens on the driver's side."

Wow! The friend's words communicated his status clearly, efficiently, and creatively. And they promoted curiosity. This brilliant, concise response implies a lot and demonstrates the power of dialogue. To deliver your own impressive dialogue, consider these techniques:

- Avoid greetings and small talk. All dialogue should be new and relevant and have a reason to be there. Use it to move the story forward.

- Make speech realistic, but not too much so. Leave out the *ums* and *ahs,* small talk, and irrelevant details.

- Make dialogue succinct and as short as possible. Long episodes of dialogue wear out readers.

- Don't let any one person speak too long.

- Pleasant conversation isn't interesting. Introduce conflict, action, emotion, vital information, or information that moves the story along.

- To vary pace, place dialogue between action, narration, and description.

- Avoid overdoing dialogue. Reserve it for significant culminating moments.

- Give each character a different "voice" so readers can tell them apart by what they say.

- Go light with regional dialects. Readers skip hard-to-read dialogue.

- People usually speak in simple sentences, even fragments. Keep compound or complex sentences to a minimum in conversation.

- Grammar rules do not apply to dialogue. People don't speak with perfect grammar.

- Use proper dialogue format and punctuation.

- Start a new paragraph each time the speaker changes.

- Use dialogue tags (he said/she said) effectively and efficiently. (See "Dialogue Tags" at the end of this chapter.)

- To test for flow, clarity, and ease of reading, read dialogue aloud.

Make certain each character's dialogue immediately distinguishes him from others, as is done in the following dialogue between two women:

Stella frowned. "Percy looks like one of those intellectually bankrupt rednecks who catches catfish with his hands."

"He's got a swagger that's kinda cute," Bee said.

"Are you kidding? That's a stagger. He walks like a squirrel drunk on fermented berries."

"I feel sorry for him. Are we trollops for interpreting the mooning incident as funny? Have we lost our dignity?"

"Yes. A toast to no dignity."

"We will still be friends with him, right?"

WHEN TO USE DIALOGUE

No one wants to read a story made up entirely of dialogue. It's equivalent to eating a dozen cookies.

Make all conversation meaningful and valuable to the story—no conversation for conversation's sake. Use dialogue to:

- Get information out in a bite-sized way.

- Interrupt narration and make less exciting information more palatable.

- Reveal characters' thoughts and interpretations.

- Express conflict or harmony.

- Move a story forward.

- Clarify.

- Reveal backstory and foreshadow future events

- Define relationships.

- Describe characters' ways of being in the world.

- Show, don't tell.

- Use characters' emotions to make the reader feel.

- Have a character obsess over something.

- Be careful with slang words in dialogue. They can date a piece—or the author.

Do all of the above, and you will know that dialogue is *the bomb*. I mean *woke*. (I'm trendy.)

****

EXAMPLE OF EFFECTIVE DIALOGUE

Dialogue does a lot of work in my short story, "The Rally." It describes characters, distinguishes them from each other, defines their relationship, and reveals their thoughts. It also moves the story forward, hints at backstory, foreshadows the future, and promotes curiosity. Accomplishing all that without dialogue would be less interesting to the reader. Note that everything said is germane to the storyline.

"You and Travis have only known each other a few months. Don't you think you should put more time in on this relationship before committing?" Jade asked.

"No. I'm good," Blaze responded. "He's the one. You know how I know? He said he'd fight a bear for me. Not a grizzly bear or one of those black bears, but you know, one of those Care Bears."

"Ha. Have you washed his truck yet?"

"No. But last weekend he washed my car, gassed it up, checked the oil and tire pressure, charged my phone, and played me a Pink Floyd love song on his guitar."

"There is no such thing as a Pink Floyd love song."

"Maybe it was Phish, then."

"You're a mess. I support whatever you decide. I'm going to miss my run-around buddy, though. I'm missing you already. Things will never be the same."

"We'll always be friends, but you're right. After the wedding, the prowling days will be over. I know, that for you, this will be another loss. I worry about you, but there's a sureness about you that wasn't there before. Bodie did you a favor with his betrayal."

Jade agreed. "I know. Now that I've adjusted, I'm glad it happened. I just wish it had happened differently. Forgiveness has settled in, though. I rarely think about him, and when I do, I don't have any feelings. It's not a void, but rather, a neutral thing. I imagine Bodie, burrowed into his recliner, smoking a cigar and watching *Bonanza*. Maybe not. Perhaps he's better to her than he was to me. If so, good for her. I'm just glad it's not me dealing with him anymore."

"How do you know when you've reached the point of forgiveness?" Blaze asked.

"When it doesn't hurt anymore. When you can say his name and feel nothing."

The serenity in Jade's voice comforted Blaze. She looked her friend in the eyes long and hard and then smiled as she took a sip of coffee. *Maybe she's healed enough to meet Travis.* "I think we girls should have one last single-girl hurrah at the dance hall before my wedding."

* * *

"Would you like to dance, darlin'?" someone asked.

Jade turned to discover a vision of cowboy glory— black hat, Wrangler jeans, tailored pearl-snap shirt, and a belt studded with silver.

She got a whiff of Stetson cologne as they walked to the dance floor. As the cowboy navigated through the crowd floor like a fine quarter horse working cattle, he said, "My name is Travis. What's yours?"

Blaze watched and smiled.

EXAMPLE OF EMOTION IN DIALOGUE

It's important that characters change over time and that their feelings are exposed in a story. In the example below, Uncle Skillet's wife was visited by his nephew (the narrator) soon after Skillet's death. Skillet was a beloved, colorful character who justified swear words by calling them "sentence enhancers." In the interest of propriety, he made up nonsensical ones in the presence of children.

An imaginative jokester, Skillet spray-painted plumes on pampas grass by the road in front of his trailer an iridescent pink color. He directed curious passersby seeking seeds to the paint section of the local hardware store.

His wife, Weezie, was in a constant state of rescuing him from his antics but always maintained he had a good heart and that his quirky ways were a gift. Following is a scene presented from the nephew's point of view.

No longer under the shadow of Skillet's robust personality, Aunt Weezie blossomed. In a sense, she took over for him. Her chitchat became flush with zingers and tender memories. On a visit, she asked, "Remember when Skillet bought me a huge teddy bear to carry around at the fair? When anyone asked where he won it, he said, 'At Sears.'"

"Yeah. Remember when he bought Daisy one?"

"Yes. She strutted around the midway, the envy of all her little friends."

I laughed. "Remember when Skillet and we kids ran around in a hail storm with buckets on our heads?"

"Yeah, you guys were bucket-heads. All that clanging should have made you deaf. I recall the time the cat got into glue in his workshop, and Skillet picked her up. He came carrying her to the trailer because she was stuck to his hands. He couldn't open the door, so he stood out on the porch meowing. I had to cut her hair to get him loose."

Weezie sat thoughtfully for a moment and then said, "Skillet weren't the kind to go to a cock fight or to drop acid at a monster truck jam, and he never got arrested, but he sure was an ornery old SOB."

"Weezie, you swore! And what do you know about acid or monster trucks?"

"I just used a sentence enhancer is all, and you know I watch all those crime shows. And I still gets Skillet's *Jacked-Up Trucks* magazine." A pensive look followed. Her eyes watered. She said, "Skillet weren't ordinary, that's for sure."

We sat silently for a moment. My throat tightened as I fought back tears.

She asked, "Can you bring me a few of those plumes from that pampas grass you planted at your place?"

My throat clamped up so tight I couldn't swallow. Tears filled my eyes. "They're pink."

Weezie's face lit up. "Oh, I must have some." Another pause, and then she said, "Skillet's bad qualities were a gift."

"Yeah. A gift."

DIALOGUE TAGS AND BEATS

A *dialogue tag* indicates who is speaking. A *beat* indicates what that person is doing while speaking. (A beat might be an action, a thought, or a description.) Although both tags and beats identify who is speaking, they are styled and punctuated differently.

- Use *said* more than any other tag. If you do use a different one, make it a simple one, such as *asked* or *responded.* Fancy verbs in a tag are a clear sign of an amateur.

- Adding adverbs to tags, such as *he said angrily, happily,* or *softly,* often appears amateurish. In general, it is best to avoid doing so. They can distract from the dialogue. Express emotion through what is said rather than a tag.

- In two-way conversations, eliminate tags where possible after the first time both people have spoken.

- Tags can be before, after, or in the middle of a quote.
    - John said, "I'm out of here."
    - "I'm out of here," John said.
    - "I'm out of here," John said, "but I'll be back."

- *Said* may be placed before or after the speaker's name.
    - "I'm out of here," John said. (modern)
    - "I'm out of here," said John. (dated but not wrong)

- Placing tags after a quote is most common. However, an up-front tag often works best if a beat is used, or if the dialogue is especially long, or if the quote is in response to a question when you could say, "Daniel responded, . . ."

- Use action words in beats. (Beats usually work best in front of what is said, and they are followed by a period.):

Cassy frowned. "Short hair? That's a deplorable thought. I'd look like a giraffe with a toupee."

David took a deep breath. "She fell down the stairs, and I called her 'safe.' I know. I know. That was just wrong. Do you think she'll go out with me again?"

Frankie stared down her son. "I told you not to go to Tijuana."

- For the most part, avoid such descriptive words as *snarled* and *gasped*, and for heaven's sake, whatever you do, don't use *hissed*. Snakes and opossums hiss. Cats hiss. People don't hiss or, if they do, stay away from them. People may grumble, but they don't growl or bark either. Mostly, they just say things.

- Start a new paragraph when the person talking changes.

- Identify who is speaking by how they talk and act.

- To test for flow and reading ease, read dialogue aloud.

PUNCTUATING DIALOGUE TAGS

- A comma is used between dialogue and the tag.

- A period is used after a beat.

- Periods and commas go inside quotation marks.

- When a tag interrupts a quote, it is set off by commas. The first letter of the second half of the sentence is in lower case: "As a matter of fact," Rex said, "consider me a serious, dedicated cyberslacker."

- If two complete sentences are involved, put a period after *said* and start the second sentence with a capital letter: "I am serious," Rex said. "The next time the system goes down, I'm playing Solitaire with a deck of cards."

It is perfectly okay to write garbage—as long as you edit brilliantly.—C. J. Cherryh

Chapter 7

REVIEW PROCESSES—
REVISION, EDITING, AND PROOFING

*If an editor or a critic labels your
work a catastrophic doozy, heal like a
fury and write your magnum opus.*

For a writer, finding an error in an already published book
is like finding a tarantula in the bathtub. Every author can
relate to that because every book has mistakes, even those
published by major companies. There are so many ways
words can dance on a page that preventing errors is
almost impossible. Why? Because the alphabet consists of
26 letters from which a writer creates a 100,000-word,
300-page book. That explains why it is impossible to
create the perfect book. But you should try.

If polishing a manuscript makes you feel as though
someone is doing a Riverdance in your head, you are not
alone. But it is the writer's job to supply the shine that
only revision, editing, and proofreading can deliver.
Don't assume these functions are what someone else
does. If a writer takes no part in them, he will struggle to
produce quality work. Stephen King said, "To write is

human, to edit is divine." A shrewd writer knows review processes are intrinsic functions of writing, and he performs editing functions himself before sending a manuscript to anyone else for their refinement.

It takes numerous reviews of a draft to get a piece good enough for someone else to review it. Here are two things a writer should never do:

(1)   Never give an unpolished manuscript to anyone.

(2)   Never submit a work for publication that has not been reviewed by another set of eyes.

REVIEW PROCESSES DEFINED

I can't write five words but that I change seven.—Dorothy Parker

The distinction between the review processes of revision, editing, and proofreading is blurred. Experts and writers use them interchangeably, sometimes perform them concurrently, and define them differently. For the purpose of this book, I'm cutting through the clutter and defining these processes by how I apply them.

Revising: This is done by the author *after the first draft*. The purpose of revision is not to identify errors, although any found are generally noted and corrected. Revision ensures what is written matters. Through it, a theme often emerges organically.

Revision considers structure and how language is used. This involves a review of flow, clarity, creative content, and the order of things. It also addresses writing style. Revision is comprehensive

102

—ranging from overview and concept evaluations down to paragraph, sentence, and word levels. It even involves rewriting.

A developmental process through which voice, style, humor, and details are enhanced, revision is where incorrect, uninteresting, and awkward material—writing similar to a truck that runs like a sewing machine—are identified and corrected. Bland writing can't do the job.

Some writers hate this process. Some don't do it. Some think someone else should do it for them. What these writers fail to realize is that *revision is writing*. It's the writer's job. It is not a chore. It is the essence of writing well. I get high on revision. It's my favorite part of the writing process because it adds depth and substance. Every run-through of a draft makes the writing shine more intensely.

During revision, the reviewer considers these qualities: In fiction, does the writing clearly communicate the story? Does the language express emotion and tone? Does it effectively describe setting, the behavior of characters, and action? Are themes and messages communicated? In nonfiction, the reviewer asks if the information is accurate, clear, orderly, concise, and precise? In every genre, the reviewer asks whether or not proper writing practices and principles are applied? Is the writing well-organized, fluid, and readable?

Components of the revision process are broad. To get a feel for them, look at the steps in the "Run-Through Layering Process" in the Appendix.

Editing: This is performed by both the author and an editor *after revision*. Some editors categorize editing functions into such terms as content editing, copyediting, and line-item editing. And they may include proofreading under the editing umbrella as well. These terms are confusing. Although I've researched editing from several sources, definitive definitions for each label have eluded me. To bring clarity to the untidiness of the definitions, I describe editing as an autopsy of a book.

The objectives of a professional edit can vary significantly. Some editors merely address flaws on a technical level and focus on industry standards. Others review syntax, semantics, mechanics, and format. Still others go deep and analyze structure, verify facts, eliminate inconsistencies, and evaluate the writing craft.

Regardless of how editing is broken down, when you, as the author, are self-editing, be concerned with all these things. Team up with your editor and address flaws on a technical level. Make certain what is written meets industry standards.

Proofreading: This is performed by the author and an editor or proofreader, *just before publication.* A correction process, proofreading is focused mostly on such details as grammar, spelling, punctuation, and formatting. The primary goal is to eliminate distracting errors that influence the perception of the author's proficiency. In the Appendix, the "Find-and-Fix Sweeps Process*"* and the "Grammar Rules and Writing Principles*"* show common errors identified during proofreading.

BETA READS: A beta read is another review process, usually performed when the manuscript is fully developed, edited, and proofed. It might even be in the galley copy stage (when the manuscript has been transformed into a bound book for final proofing). Writers, readers (audience members), and friends are candidates for such reviews. Beta reads focus primarily on the construct of a book and the overall effectiveness of the writing rather than editing details

A writer needs to integrate himself into the writer community to have access to effective beta readers. Tapping into those who specialize in the same genre is generally best. Friends as beta readers can be problematic. They will typically love, love, love what you wrote. Whomever you use, give them a list of questions:

- What is the strongest chapter? The weakest?

- What's your favorite part? Your least favorite?

- If I took a chapter out, which would you suggest?

- Was anything confusing or unbelievable?

- Was there any portion you wanted to skip?

- Were settings appropriate and visually portrayed?

- Did you like the characters? Were they believable?

- In a three-sentence review, what would you say?

This tactic may or may not work. Most likely, friendly reviewers will still love, love, love what you wrote.

It's not unusual for someone to take a long time to do a beta read, if they complete the task at all. For this reason, many writers pay beta readers and set agreed-to completion dates. I've been paid $100 several times for doing them. It's a generous act for someone to do a beta read. Thank them and include the person in the book's Acknowledgements.

PROFESSIONALISM: Novice writers often assume that after three or four drafts, their work is good to go to an editor. Perhaps established authors who are masterful writing geniuses and have major publishers to polish their work can pull that off. But most writers produce many drafts and self-edit over and over before their work is ready for another set of eyes.

It's unprofessional to deliver an unpolished composition to anyone. When I coach writers, I struggle to give quality feedback when the composition is a mess. If you aspire to be a sharp, respected author—a professional—you will work toward being a self-editing aficionado.

VALIDITY OF ADVICE: Some writing requirements are controversial. For example, my editors disagree over the use of the word "that." One takes them out. The other puts them in. I value both perspectives and, as a result of their disparate preferences, I find a nice balance. When there is controversy, pick a method and be consistent in its application.

Some editing suggestions are highly subjective or contrary to the author's perspective. No one knows the subject and style of a piece, or the approach to creating it, better than the author. Sharp editors typically dig deep into details and are generous with advice, but as the creator, trust your judgment on whether or not to take it.

COSTS OF EDITING AND PROOFREADING: A broad range of billing options exist, including: charging by word, by page, or a flat fee. Professional editors might run $1,500 per book. I've hired one for $2 a page, about $500 per book. I've also spent a couple of thousand on editing a book. Each author must decide the financial investment he is willing to make. Whatever the cost, money spent on editing might be the best investment a writer ever made.

Before submitting my book to an editor, I self-edit it *at least* five times. Yes, five. (I'm not obsessive.) Still, I find errors. I delivered to my editor what I believed was a perfect book. She returned it with 106 errors. I accepted all but two. Since then, when I deliver a book to her, I tell her it is perfect, and she smiles at me like a Cheshire cat.

REVIEW CHALLENGES

This morning I took out a comma and this afternoon I put it back again.—Oscar Wilde

When you reach the point Wilde describes, it is probably time to go to print. The following describes my path to producing a book. I hope at least parts of it will work for you. But keep in mind, I'm obsessive. Find your own process. Let's begin with some general information.

SPELLING AND GRAMMAR CHECKERS: An over reliance on either of these tools can spell trouble. They are no substitute for editing. Spell check is a fickle friend. If you say *sour* instead of *soar*, *sweat* instead of *sweet*, *mustard* instead of *mustered*, or *economic* instead of *ergonomic*, it is not going to catch the error. Trust me. I know. And grammar checkers can mislead as well.

To help identify errors, some experts suggest reading a manuscript backward, which forces a writer to look at each word as distinct from the meaning of the sentence. This does reveal certain types of errors; however, it is a burdensome process that is impractical for a book. I would worry about a person who has the fortitude to read an entire book backward.

FORMATTING

Formatting is not a pretty process, but it must be done.

Normally, a book is produced in two phases.

- **Manuscript format** is 8 1/2 x 11 inches, double spaced, single-sided pages (front only), and left justified text alignment.

- **Book format** is smaller, usually 6 x 9 inches, single spaced, two-sided pages (front and back), and left and right justified text alignment.

Under the traditional publishing model, writers deliver a book in manuscript format to agents and, ultimately, a publisher converts it into book format for printing.

Authors like myself, who self-publish (and are not seeking an agent or publisher), are responsible for reformatting from manuscript to book format. For this reason, I skip manuscript format and write directly into book format. This saves time by eliminating the conversion process, and it allows me to see my work in its final form as I'm writing it. (My editors are okay with editing from book format. Not all would be.)

I do self-edits before delivering a book to my editors so it is as clean as I can get it. This includes two separate processes: one for editing the format and one for the text. Editing processes are different for each. (Editing tips are included at the end of this chapter. And format and text editing checklists are included at the end of the next chapter.)

Even after all this self-editing, my editors find plenty of things that need fixing. When I turn a manuscript over to them, my brilliance astounds me. When I get it back, I'm humbled. That is the nature of the process. To avoid discouragement, remember that collaborative editing is the most profound, lucrative learning experience you can have. And it produces a beautiful book. Team up with your editor.

After all this self-editing and editing is finished, I'm sick to death of my book. I get over that quickly, though, when I see it on Amazon and hold a copy in my hands. It's a beauty.

FIXING PUBLISHED ERRORS: Fortunately, when an imperfection is found in either text or format after publication, and the writer is using a print-on-demand vendor, a corrected file can be sent to the printer, and the next book printed will include those fixes.

WRITER CAMARADERIE: We writers are all having the same experiences. As a member of the writer community, champion others by giving online reviews and providing feedback on errors found while reading each other's published books. When I find errors in the books of writers I know well, I send them an email asking if they want input. I appreciate it when they do the same for me.

An essential part of the review process is evaluating word use and eliminating unnecessary words. The following example illustrates the value of performing a review, or run-through, focused on this crucial aspect of writing craft—writing efficiently.

ELIMINATING EXCESS WORDS

When Thoreau wrote: "Simplify, simplify, simplify!" shouldn't he have edited it down to "Simplify!"?—Cranky Pappy

One of the most common mistakes rookie writers make is not writing efficiently. Thomas Jefferson said, "The most valuable of all talents is that of never using two words when one will do." Evaluate every word. Look for opportunities to replace words with more interesting or descriptive ones. Eliminate overused and trite words, and your work will blossom.

The following example contains words that newbie writers, who have not studied craft, tend to use unnecessarily or excessively. Note how much better and stronger the writing is when unnecessary or inappropriate words are eliminated during the revision process.

Overuse of Adverbs and Adjectives

My dad was an **extremely** conscientious man with a **very** strong, **unwavering** work ethic. He worked **really** hard. An **incredibly** responsible family man, he brought in a **very** steady wage.

Edited: My dad was a conscientious man with a strong work ethic. He worked hard and brought in a steady wage.

Overuse of Adjectives and *Would* (a verb tense issue)

Dad **would** get up **very** early on **every** winter morning and start a **roaring** fire to warm the house. Mom **would** be fixing breakfast and yelling at **all** us kids, "Everybody up!" We **would** wake up to the smell of **delicious** frying bacon. **All** five of us **would** tumble downstairs, clothes in hand, to dress by the heat of the **roaring** fire while turning like chickens on rotisseries.

Edited: Dad got up early on winter mornings to build a fire to warm the house. Mom fixed breakfast while yelling at us kids, "Everybody up!" We woke up to the smell of frying bacon. Five of us tumbled downstairs, clothes in hand, to dress by a fire so hot we turned like chickens on rotisseries.

Overuse of Adjectives and *Had* (a verb tense issue)

I **had** started school, so Mom **had** sewed-up new clothes for me. The fabric was **usually** calico or something of that sort. **All** the girls in my class **were wearing pretty**, store-bought dresses their mothers **had gotten** for them, and they **had** more than one pair of shoes. So I **had gotten** off to a bad start and **had** no friends until I **had** met **my friend** Sherry.

Edited: When I started school, Mom sewed new clothes for me. The fabric was calico or something of that sort. The girls in my class wore store-bought dresses and had more than one pair of shoes. So I got off to a bad start and had no friends until I met Sherry.

For more details on eliminating unnecessary words, refer to the "Find-and-Fix Sweeps Process" in the Appendix. The following list of editing tips and the next chapter expand further on the review processes of revision, editing, and proofreading.

****

EDITING TIPS

When you think your document is perfect, proof it again. You will find it is not. Repetitive review processes are required to produce a clean, honed copy to be delivered to an editor. When you reach the point of changing things back and forth, it's time to move on. This is after you've done considerable revision, self-editing, and proofreading. Approach review with the assumption there are errors, and you are going to find them. Here are some editing tips:

- Put the manuscript aside for a week or so before editing or proofreading.

- Edit and proofread only when mentally alert. If you're not finding mistakes, you may be missing them. Take a break.

- Proofread from hard copy. Read slowly and out loud as though reading to an audience. This reveals awkward flow, and you'll hear mistakes you won't see on a computer screen.

- Use a red pen to note changes so you can easily spot them when making fixes. Double-check fixes.

- Zoom in on the computer. Proofread word by word from this larger print.

- Edit out echoes (words repeated over and over). Authors tend to overuse certain words. Also, avoid repeating important words in the same paragraph. And don't use an uncommonly expressive word more than two or three times in a book (examples: *pizzazz, savvy, extraordinary*).

- Proof everything. Don't ignore formatting (page numbers, headers, footers, titles, spacing, etc.).

- Proof format separately from the text (the processes are different for each).

- Do a run-through focused solely on eliminating unnecessary words and sentences. Be brutal, and the writing will be better. (When I reduce word count to meet contest requirements, the pieces are always stronger.)

- Do a run-through putting every word on trial. Eliminate adverbs and stacked adjectives. Search for bland words and replace them with more interesting or more descriptive ones. (Don't overdo.)

- Review chapters out of order. Read complicated chapters first, while you're fresh, or start from the last chapter and work backward.

- Review each paragraph. Assess sentence order. In general, make certain the first sentence is topical, the last one clarifies or sums up the paragraph and transitions to the next one, and all sentences are relevant and not redundant.

- Read from the perspective of your harshest critic. Neutralize his criticism where possible. This often results in changes that make a difference in content and tone.

- After making all corrections, double-check them. Verify their influence on page numbers, chapter breaks, table of contents, index, etc. (You will cause errors in the process of fixing them.)

- Use a two-day process on newly written pieces, especially for submissions. You will discover something you missed on day one that needs fixing or improvement on day two.

Rewrite, rewrite, rewrite, don't be precious about your first draft, . . . be your own worst critic, confront your weakness and remember writing is a craft.—Tobsha Learner

Chapter 8

HOW TO PRODUCE
THE *ALMOST* PERFECT BOOK

Half my life is an act of revision.—John Irving

I say the *almost* perfect book because, although a writer aspires to achieve perfection, it is unlikely he will do so. If you are determined to reread your book until you find no errors, good luck with that. You will find errors, or at least needed improvements, every time. At some point, you must stop the madness, abandon the quest for perfection, and go to print. Although it's unlikely you will ever produce the perfect book, set that as a goal anyway.

It is rare to read a book that doesn't have errors in it, even one produced by major publishers. As frustrating as this is for a writer, the important thing is that his book exists, not that it is perfect. Nevertheless, you want your book to be as polished as possible.

Thinking you were careful and don't need someone to review what you wrote is naivety squared. It's like believing your dog is vegetarian. Read it one more time, and you will think differently. After that, if you read it again, you will find even more errors. I have never read one of my books without finding something wrong—ever.

LESSONS LEARNED: Proofreading was the most tedious, challenging, and frustrating part of producing my books, other than using technology. I eventually licked the technology issue—sort of. I didn't win in the proofreading arena. I found errors in every book after it was published.

After publishing my first book, I printed a large quantity of them, a costly mistake that carried with it tremendous disappointment. But I learned two lessons:

(1) Don't order large quantities of books. Order just enough to meet immediate needs. You don't want a hundred shredder-bound books sitting around with errors in them. Thirty—not so bad.

(2) If you tweak the manuscript after it's edited, you risk creating errors.

Hint: After changing something in the text, proofread the paragraph twice. Review the one before and after it. Check for wording or formatting issues caused by the change, including those in the table of contents and the index. One change can affect many things.

(3) Always have the cover proofed.

I have not acquired the self-discipline to stop tweaking my books after they've been edited by someone else. Although I've come to realize I'm not painting a Monet, I can't control the urge to make last-minute changes. No lessons learned the hard way have quieted this obsession. If I were a child, I would be put in time-out.

Errors discovered in my books after publication made me feel like a special kind of stupid, although they were not the result of a lack of effort. I had three people edit my last book. Each found valid, but often different, mistakes. When I read it one last time, I found six more. After it was published, I found three more. I'm certain if I read it again, I'd find more. Thanks to print-on-demand, these errors were corrected, and a revised electronic file submitted before the next book was printed.

Perhaps the following thought will be some consolation when you must cope with errors: Most likely, you will never get the perfect book, but you will be in good company when you don't get it.

SELF-EDITS

I'm not a very good writer, but I'm an excellent rewriter.—James A. Michener

The wise writer invests considerable time and effort in revision, editing, and proofreading before delivering his work to anyone else. Consider revision as part of the writing process rather than as an aftermath. I spend more time on revision than on writing, and I use the following review processes (illustrated in the Appendix):

- Run-Through Layering Process

- Find-and-Fix Sweeps Process

- Grammar Rules and Writing Principles Edit

When planning out a timeline for producing a book, I allow a year or two for the layering process (it is part of revision, which *is* writing). It's not unusual for me to go over my manuscript thirty or more times during this revision process. On my first book, I stopped counting at sixty.

Then I plan on "at least" three months for review functions (editing). Following is the editing timeline:

- The first month is me—self-editing.

- The second is editors, proofreaders, and beta readers reviewing, and me—self-editing again. (This may take twice this amount of time.)

- The third is me—fixing and double checking the fixes. Then, I do one more final edit.

Note my involvement in all three stages. Not doing intense self-edits makes as much sense as giving a person directions to pick you up at the corner of *Walk* and *Don't Walk*. You are unlikely to get where you want to go. (Self-editing steps are illustrated at the end of this chapter.)

Whether or not you take time to do all the steps proposed here is a personal choice. But keep in mind that errors annoy readers. Although Kingsley Amis was talking about content when he said, "If you can't annoy somebody, there is little point in writing," you probably don't want to irritate readers with writing errors. Content—maybe.

It might be helpful to consider editing as having five stages within this three-month process, which is what I do:

FIRST MONTH

Stage I - Self-Edit: This is the editing process I described in the previous chapter. I have this grand illusion that, through that process, I'm going to impress my editors. But they always find plenty of errors. It's humbling. Still, my goal is to deliver a polished product to them. So I review my book over and over.

The format and the text are edited separately because the process for each is different. The goal is to find all errors. Since that never happens, after about five passes, I surrender. (The steps to this self-editing process are listed at the end of this chapter.)

SECOND MONTH

Stage II - Editing/Proofreading: I deliver a copy of my manuscript electronically in Word or in hard copy to editors. (Most writers give their books to editors in manuscript format. I don't.*) Each editor has a different area of expertise, and each finds different things. I do another edit, myself, while waiting for their input. The results of all these edits are put into my computerized manuscript file and double-checked for accuracy.

Stage III - Beta Readers: Through Kindle Direct Publishing (KDP Amazon Publishing), my printer, I transform my book's computerized file into a *bound proof* book (called a *galley proof* in the industry). I order a galley copy for beta readers and one for myself. For this review step, I'm looking for input from seasoned writers and my reading audience on writing technique—what works, what docsn't, and obvious crrors. Unfortunately, this review process may reveal needed rewrites that require editing. I decide which changes to accept, make those changes to the manuscript file, and order a final galley proof from my printer.

---

*Because I self-publish and am not pursuing agents and publishers, I skip the manuscript format they require and write books directly into print format for a 6x9-inch book. If you are writing in manuscript format, you will not have a bound proof copy for Stages II and III.

THIRD MONTH

Stage IV - Final Edit: From this final proof, I review both the cover and the text one last time, knowing I will find errors even after all those reviews. I make fixes, double-check them, and perhaps pay for a final proofreading. That means I've used three editors, at least two beta readers, and two proofreaders.

Stage V - Post-Publication Review: Once the book is *live* on Amazon, I order a copy to test the reader experience. I sit curled up on the sofa and read the book for pleasure, as though I am a reader. Guess what? I find errors, usually several. For this reason, I don't announce the publication of the book or schedule a book launch until I've had time to do this final, post-publication process and send in a revised file to Amazon.

COPING WITH IMPERFECTION

I wrote asses instead of assess. I wrote voluptuous instead of voluminous. I used tart instead of start. But it was using pubic, instead of public, on a billboard that took the problem to a whole new level.

Okay, okay, the billboard thing didn't happen, but it does illustrate potential consequences of blunders. When you discover an imperfection in something already published, know that such errors are *the hand of man.* Give thanks for print-on-demand, which allows you to fix mistakes before the next book is printed. And apply this coping tactic: a well-timed, "Oh, well." (I talk a good game, but errors in my books traumatize me, and I've never gotten over that.)

****

SELF-EDITING CHECKLIST

Format Checklist

These steps apply to book format (as opposed to manuscript format). For this reason, some steps do not apply to books in manuscript format.

Setup:
____Consistent margins and margin justification
____Consistent header, footer, and page number locations

Chapters:
____Appropriate chapter section breaks and page breaks
____Chapters start on odd page numbers (right side)
____No header on first pages of chapters
____Chapter numbers/titles/subtitles are correct
____Capitalization is consistent in titles, subtitles, headers
____Spacing down to chapter numbers is consistent
____Spacing between number/title/subtitles/text is consistent
____Font size/style consistent in chapter titles and subtitles
____Chapter number/titles consistent with table of contents
____Index numbers are correct

Headers/Footers:
____Header information is consistent with chapter titles
____All page numbers in headers or footers are correct
____Font size/style and location of headers are consistent
____No headers or footers on blank pages

Page Numbers:
____Numbers flow properly throughout
____Numbers are located in same spot on each page
____No page numbers on blank pages

Indents and Spacing Features:
_____Paragraph indents are consistent
_____Text indents (usually for quotations) are consistent
_____Spaces between characters are appropriate
_____Line spacing is consistent

Table of Contents:
_____Table of Contents information matches chapters/headers
_____All page numbers are odd numbers for chapter heads
_____Title capitalization/fonts/spaces consistent with text

Text Checklist

For the text edit, proofread over and over until you find few errors. If your goal is to proof until you find no errors, well, good luck with that.

_____Dates, numbers, proper names, and cross references correct
_____Quotation marks and parentheses are paired
_____No widows (single words or lines dangling by themselves, at the beginning or ending of paragraphs or pages)
_____Structure is parallel in any series of words or phrases
_____Font size and style are consistent
_____Single spaces after periods at end of sentences
_____Questions end with question marks unless rhetorical (no answer expected)
_____All periods and commas are inside quotation marks
_____All paragraphs have ending punctuation (a missing period at the end of a paragraph is a common error)
_____Lists have consistent sentence structure and punctuation (a period after each item listed, or not)

_____Consistent use of capitalization and punctuation on lists and headings, as well as in entire text

_____Tone and content reflect vision and purpose

Corrections: Double-check any corrections made. Reread the entire paragraph in which a change was made twice. Check the influence of that change on previous and subsequent paragraphs, as well as on page numbers, chapter breaks, the table of contents, and the index.

Final-Reading Checklist

_____Take a break. Put the book aside. Let it bake before doing another run-through. Read it fresh when you are alert.

_____Read after using the software feature that reveals the invisible formatting marks for spaces, tabs, paragraphs, and section breaks.

_____Read from a larger print (zoom in). Mistakes not noticed with smaller print will pop out.

_____Read the manuscript aloud to evaluate the pace and flow of the language. This strategy reveals awkward sentence structure. Check that rhythm is incorporated, while unintended, repetitive sentence structures are avoided.

_____Read the manuscript from the perspective of others, including your harshest critic. Polish it so it's difficult for that person, or anyone else, to challenge anything in it.

_____Read the published book for fun. Pretend you are a member of your audience.

This checklist illustrates why it is a severe challenge to get a perfect book. But as I've said before, you should try.

Memoirist Peter Selgin said, "When my mother read my memoir, my greatest fear was that she would be hurt by the suggestions that, as a teenager during World War II, she had anti-Semitic sentiments. No. What offended her was a description of our house in disrepair. . . ."—Jack Smith, *The Writer* magazine, August 2019.

Chapter 9

THE IMPERTINENCE OF CRITIQUE

Asking a working writer what he thinks about critics is like asking a lamp-post what it feels about dogs. —John Osborne

You cannot predict what will offend someone, and there will always be someone who doesn't like something you wrote. Occasionally, that person lacks the sensitivity gene. Don't let criticism spiral you into an existential crisis. Hey, you wrote something. That's killer. Revel in that.

Critique groups provide incredibly efficient learning opportunities. You'll learn as much from observing the critique of other writers' work as from feedback on your own.

A writer's success depends, in part, on how well he deals with criticism. Although it's hard to take, it is an incubator for the evolution of a composition, and it might keep a writer out of trouble. Critique groups have saved me on several occasions.

I wrote a textbook on aging for a university-sponsored workshop for older folks and worked hard to keep this tough subject upbeat and positive. However, in the Introduction, while making a case for why the book was important, I exposed the downsides of aging in the first few paragraphs. A critique group in a college course I took called me on this. "Who would want to read about such a depressing topic?" they asked. How could I have missed that? I was so focused on explaining why the book was important that I ensured no one would want to read it. I had massacred its upbeat message of how to age in a way that is a gift to others.

Unnoticed flaws are often exposed through critique, such as too-long paragraphs, organizational issues, confusing information, awkward flow, and irrational content. Critique members are particularly good at identifying where to start a story, an essay, a poem, or a nonfiction book.

I've learned more, and learned it most efficiently, from critics than from any other source other than editors. In particular, intense critiquing experiences in five-day workshops at the University of Iowa's Summer Writing Festival and at William Bernhardt's retreats resulted in major enhancements to my writing. I highly recommend both of these sessions.

Many educational institutions and well-known authors offer such workshops. It's best to seek one in your genre; however, let me qualify that statement. I've been the only nonfiction writer in a couple of workshops, and I learned from the fiction writers. I believe they also learned from me, as explained in *the gender bounce* mentioned earlier.

EDITING AS CRITIQUE: Editing is a form of critique. Susan Bell alluded to the scale of the editing process in *The Artful Edit* when she said, "While we write into a void, we edit into a universe." This winsome thought suggests editing is somehow important in the grand scheme of things. Although I question such resplendent, universal implications, no doubt, editing is a critical component of critique. Make your editor your wingman. Learn what she knows.

CRITIQUE AS A SKILLSET: Critiquing is a skill. Serious writers will invest in building that skill. Being good—really good—at giving and receiving feedback is a valuable writing capability. It's a measure of authorship. It is also an important role that ensures a writer is "a player" in the world of writing.

To be a skillful critique group participant, always stay positive. Point out a section that needs work by suggesting it be brought up to the level of more polished parts. Instead of saying you didn't like something, say "I noticed." Never say, "I disagree." Instead, ask a questions, "Did you consider. . .?" Be your compadres' champion.

Focus on evaluating global issues, such as tone, overall theme, and the validity of concepts. Note what can be cut, further developed, or moved around. Evaluate beginnings for potency and consider whether or not the work starts at the right place. Look for punch in endings so pieces end strong.

Although I cannot truthfully portray critique as enjoyable, I do consider it a requirement of my profession. And I know that the better I am at it, the better writer I will be. As tough as it is to receive critique (I experience considerable angst about it before hand), I have always been exceedingly thankful afterward that I sought it out.

CRITIQUE GROUPS: Two common types of critique groups are: (1) those composed of writing associates, and (2) those that are part of workshops or classes. Both types function as effective sounding boards and are a lucrative source of ideas. Writers are often shocked at what fresh eyes notice in their works. An astute writer values candid feedback and, as a bonus, enjoys the camaraderie of interaction with other writers through critique activities.

The talent, knowledge, and composition of the group determines its effectiveness. Some groups click. Some don't. Setting an end-date up front on a group's existence allows for diplomatically starting over with a new group.

CRITIQUE PARTNERS: Such groups often include writers from multiple genres and with varying skill levels. Although, it is generally best to partner with others in your genre and with your level of expertise or higher, input from diverse and unseasoned writers can be helpful since it is likely to reflect average reader perspectives.

The power of craft comes from writers being elegant in their weirdness. Authors need editors and critique partners who celebrate that weirdness while having the pluck to call them out when they take it too far.

The last thing you need is a timid, kindly person critiquing your work. You need a tough old bird like me. You don't need a tactless know-it-all, either. Whatever the risks, be brave, seek input from any source, and take it in.

COPING WITH CRITIQUE

Like the green patina on copper that many consider beautiful, errors in a composition can be viewed as patina. They are part of the natural order of things because errors are a result of the hand of man.

If you don't want candid feedback, do not bring your composition to a critique group. If you do seek critique, don't expect only praise. Put your work out there, brace yourself, and take your hits. You need to know, from different perspectives, what works and what doesn't. Such information is a windfall. You don't have to agree with suggestions. Listen, and then do what you want.

Ideally, your book is well-developed and polished before you pursue critique, but even then, critique partners will find plenty to point out. I have learned not to sit at the critique table all confident and arrogant thinking the group is going to be wowed by my work. Always, they nail my butt. Slowly, my pallor changes, and I need a Snickers. So brace yourself and take in the feedback. Thank your partners, go home and heal, and then do your own thing your way.

Avoid being defensive in critique settings, or anywhere else for that matter, especially when it comes to reviews. A character in Orson Scott Card's book, *Alvin Journeyman*, took issue with someone's critique. Although the character was not diplomatic, he was exceptionally eloquent:

> And if you're going to criticize me for not finishing the whole thing and tying it up in a bow for you, why, do us both a favor and write your own damn book, only have the decency to call it a romance instead of a history, because history's got no bows on it, only frayed ends of ribbons and knots that can't be untied. It ain't a pretty package, but then, it's not your birthday, that I know of, so I'm under no obligation to give you a gift.

In general, defensive reactions to critique are best avoided. Writers are under no obligation to "sell" their positions, but it is prudent to remain openminded and consider that a critic might be right. If he didn't "get" a writer's perspective, readers may not, either. So at the critique table, just listen and accept feedback.

It's best not to respond to critical comments or reviews either, especially on the Internet. Doing so can lead to public conflict, as do so many interactions on social media. On the other hand, a "thank you" for a good review or suggestion would surely be appreciated.

FLAWS AS PATINA: If a writer's work is messy, people have a hard time taking him seriously; however, achieving perfection is something with which every writer struggles. Most readers recognize that. Don't be like me and fret obsessively over imperfections. Fix them if you can, and then move on. When feedback makes you feel bad, consider self-talk coping tactics, such as *whatever*; *roll with it*; *this, too, shall pass; stay the course*; and *oh, well.*

The important thing is that you created something. In doing so, you gave a gift, one that will last for generations. Celebrate that. Be like the crazy-ass character in one of my stories who said to a friend who did something incredible, "That's stupid wonderful. Makes me feel so pedestrian in comparison. Let's go get you a tattoo."

ENDURANCE: In my business book, *Leadership Savvy*, I wrote about five keys to career success. One of those was endurance. Like most writers, I've experience burnout and contemplated quitting. However, that's not a viable option for me. Creating through writing is an obsession that churns like a cyclone in my head. That storm makes me happy. Criticism occasionally dampens my spirit and causes me to take a break, but I always come back.

Successful writers are amateurs who didn't quit. My wish for you is that you endure, that you find your own special niche in the world of writing, and that you brazenly open yourself up to critique and bask in the self-improvement it fosters. As you unleash your creative spirit, be assured that you will be a better writer because you collaborated and took in the contributions of others.

****

CRITIQUE CRITERIA

It is best if a critique group determines some operational criteria up front. This means agreeing on optimal meeting times, frequency, location, processes, format, page limits, and critique rules. Comply diligently with requirements. Avoid submitting more than your share of pages for critique.

Critiquing is a skill—a valuable, purposeful one you can be proud of mastering. Be constructive when providing feedback. Respect differing opinions. Don't impose your morals, values, or writing style on others. Comment on both positive and negative attributes of a piece. Find the balance between candid feedback and sensitivity so your impressions are well received.

Begin by mentioning what you love about a piece—what works well—such as beautiful phrasing, impressive creativity, profound thoughts. Then make suggestions for improvement. Look for the following:

- Lack of premise or overall theme

- Inappropriate or ineffective tone

- Points of confusion or inaccurate information

- Inadequate description or too much, particularly in regard to settings and environments

- Issues with structure, flow, or order

- Inconsistent point of view

- Beginning or ending that lacks punch

- Sagging tension or lack of conflict

- Too little or too much action

- A pace that is too slow, too fast, or doesn't vary

- Characters who are stagnant, bland, unbelievable, or not relatable (They are not learning and changing, or they are not unique or fascinating in some way. A story needs characters readers love to love or love to hate.)

- Inadequate connections between characters

- Events that are unbelievable or don't make sense

- A plot that is not intriguing or an unsatisfactory climax or resolution. (Readers need satisfaction.)

- Story evokes no emotions on the part of the reader, or unintended emotions are stirred

- Stilted dialogue or conversation that doesn't move the story forward, characters who are not distinguished by the way they talk, dialogue that doesn't give relevant information or is distracting, ineffective slang, intrusive cursing, or overpowering dialect

- Unfortunate word choices, repeated words, excess words, show-off words, words that send reader to a dictionary

- Not applying writing principles or practices

- Errors in spelling, punctuation, or grammar

- The writer has not made a connection with readers

A good critic is gentle with novice writers, open-minded about the opinions and values of others, and appreciative of those writing in genres other than his own. Most importantly, he is humble.

SECTION III

WRITING TOOLS AND PROCESSES

Writing is like driving at night in the fog. You can only see as far as your headlights, but you can make the whole trip that way.—E. L. Doctorow

Chapter 10

STRUCTURE—ORGANIZATION

Rules are made to be broken. The world doesn't need another formula book. It needs the literary equivalent of an avant-garde painting.

Effective structure is all about organization of content. It ensures that the text hooks a reader, fascinates an agent or publisher, impresses a contest judge, and keeps the manuscript out of a reject pile. Publishers are looking for something different. A wise writer asks: How can I shape my composition so it is distinctive, perhaps even remarkably idiosyncratic, without going too far?

THE ORDER OF THINGS

Every chapter and scene is a mini-story with a beginning, middle, and end.—William Bernhardt

The simplistic and common beginning-middle-end structure is appropriate for every genre. About twenty percent of a book is the setup; sixty percent, the middle; and twenty percent, the wrap-up. It's the finesse with which those spaces are filled that makes a composition unique and gives it value.

I'm mostly a nonfiction kinda gal. Writing fiction for me is like getting asked out on a date by a guy who says he's so happy to be out of prison for killing his wife, and I'm digging out the pepper spray. I've studied fiction, though, and won a few contest in the genre, so I know some stuff. The beginning hooks the reader and introduces a central theme. The middle clarifies and embellishes plots and subplots. One or more escalating conflicts or crises culminate in a climax, which is a point or an event of the greatest intensity. The end resolves the conflict, ties up loose ends, and provides satisfaction for the reader.

STRUCTURE OPTIONS

Don't be the person who says, "The plan is that there is no plan." Maybe you don't plan it all out up front, but at some point, you've got to focus on structure.

How structure is accomplished is influenced by genre and author preferences. Designing the architecture up front smooths and expedites the writing process for most writers, although some fiction writers let characters take the wheel. An outline is helpful for sequencing scenes, facilitating pacing, identifying placement of structural signposts, and ensuring rational flow and content. With nonfiction, a table of contents can serve to organize structure. Many structural alternatives exist, including:

The Narrative Arc Structure

This approach is used mostly in fiction or story-like memoir. It supports the sequencing of events. Think of it in terms of a line that starts at a point on the lower left of a graph, rises in a curve to a peak in the middle (the bulk of a story), and then drops back down again at the end.

On the continuum of the curve is rising action, complications and escalation, climax, falling action, and resolution. John Lynch describes the narrative arc as, "Boy gets Girl; Boy loses Girl; Boy gets Girl back."

Fitting scenes under the umbrella of a narrative arc ensures the story makes sense and flows in a logical progression. This prevents a critic from suggesting that the narrative is unclear or inconsistent. Robb Grindstaff said, "Your narrative arc should look like a bell curve, not a map of a suburban neighborhood full of circle drives, cul-de-sacs, and dead end roads."

Some writers post the scenes of their stories under an arc in storyboard fashion, which provides a visual before the writing starts. Others outline or build the arc as they go. However it's done, a narrative arc facilitates the writing process and organizes a story so it makes sense to the reader. Research *narrative arc* for more details.

There is nothing magical about the arc itself. A straight line visual with chapters and scenes distributed along that continuum can do the same thing as illustrated in William Bernhardt's book, *Story Structure*.

The "W" Structure

An effective storytelling framework, this approach is used in almost every television sitcom and reality show, including home makeover programs. It also works in books.

The first leg of the W (downward stroke): The program begins on a high note. Characters bond with the audience. A situation is introduced. Then, a serious problem develops, and things go downhill fast.

The second leg (upward stroke): A strategy to solve the problem is introduced, which promotes optimism and takes the situation back to a high point.

The third leg (downward stroke again): Just as this rally seems complete, a major crisis develops (right before the last commercial on a television show) that drags the situation down again. A formidable calamity of some sort fosters chaos—mold in the basement, an unfortunate haircut, the police arrive, someone is humiliated, a bug bomb kills a lizard, Dad gets sick from expired yogurt, or some other disaster. High emotion, arguments, and dissent are portrayed. The situation appears hopeless.

The last leg (upward stroke again): After the commercial, the climax delivers resolution and salvation. This takes the stroke back up to the W's top. Something saves the day and all is well: the jury speaks, characters make up, the criminal is subdued, the dog is found, or someone removes the gardenia-inspired wallpaper. A character has changed. And the show's main message becomes clear.

The Defining Event Structure

Rather than a chronological approach, this alternative uses a defining moment (a traumatic event that changes everything) or an inciting incident (intense drama or action of some sort) early on. (Usually, this happens after readers have had time to bond with the main character.) Then, the backstory leading up to that moment is introduced, followed by the after story.

Crime shows often follow this format. They show the murder up front and then go back to the history of the victim and the criminal. This is followed by the aftermath —an investigation, which ultimately leads to a trial.

Water for Elephants is an example of this approach in fiction. The inciting incident in the prologue draws in the reader. (Read this prologue on Amazon by clicking on "Look inside.") In early chapters, the backstory that led up to that event is revealed. Later, the prologue incident is replayed as part of the aftermath that leads to the climax. I would never have read a book about a circus in the early 1900s had I not read the prologue. It sucked me in.

This structure works nicely in memoirs. I used it in mine, *Red Heels and Smokin'—How I Got My Moxie Back.* Most people have had life experiences that changed everything—a turning point that redirected the trajectory of their lives. After starting with a profound experience that grabs the reader, the author reveals the backstory that led up to it and then reports the aftermath.

This approach to structure violates the traditional model of beginning, middle, and end in the chronological sense. However, as Jean Luc Godard said, "A story should have a beginning, a middle and an end, but not necessarily in that order." Rules can be broken.

PARTS OF A BOOK: Numerous components, called *front matter, body,* and *back matter,* divide up a book. Rookies tend to use the parts inappropriately, overuse them, or place them in the wrong spots. They misspell such words as *foreword* and *copyright.* Agents and publishers marvel at such blatant flaws. Use only those parts vitally needed, and use them properly. Definitions of the parts of a book are described at the end of this chapter.

PLOT VERSUS STRUCTURE: Structure and plot are not the same thing. Both are global concepts in fiction, but plot is the main character's journey—the story. Structure involves the arrangement and organization of the story—the design. Some design ideas include:

- The first person a reader meets is who he relates to most. Introduce the main character early on.

- Make the main character endearing to the audience in an early scene by how he interacts with children, animals, or the downtrodden. (There's a reason *The Big Chill* starts with parents bathing a young child.)

- Ensure that the protagonist wants something, and introduce obstacles to him getting it.

- Have the antagonist be the obstacle to the main character getting what he wants.

- Include a foil, who possesses qualities that contrast with those of the protagonist or the antagonist (like Dr. Watson and Sherlock Holmes). A foil can be a mentor, a sidekick, a love interest, a comedic henchman, or whatever.

- Create trials and tribulations. Increase the stakes. The story must always move forward. Each scene results from what happened in the one before it and influences the one that comes after it. If it does not, rewrite the scene, move it, or take it out.

- Introduce calamity and highs and lows that add oomph to a story. At some point near the end, all appears lost, just before all is saved—usually.

- Surprise readers with twists and turns—a character dies, a new one is introduced, the protagonist changes what he wants, or any other sudden shift.

- Show that the main character and others were changed, in the end, by their experiences.

- After the climax, problems and conflicts are resolved; and loose ends, tied up. Readers are made to feel good about how things turned out, or they are left tearful, pensive, or contemplative. It's important for them to feel emotion.

PREMISE VERSUS THEME

The premise is your elevator speech, one that can be given in two or three sentences.

If someone asks you what you are writing, and you can't immediately tell them in a couple of sentences, you've not written down the premise and theme of your book. Articulating them early on, guides writing and provides verbiage to explain to agents, publishers, and other curious inquirers what you are writing about.

Because premise and theme are kindred spirits, they are sometimes used interchangeably. Generally, the *premise* is the central idea of a story, expressed in one or two sentences. The *theme* is the message or meaning of the story. Research these online. (William Bernhardt's book, *Powerful Premise*, explains these terms in detail.)

In addition to providing a writer with the language to communicate the gist of his work to others, articulating the premise and theme helps keep him on track as he develops his work in progress.

****

PARTS OF A BOOK
(Use as few "optional" parts as possible.)

FRONT MATTER

Title Page: (required) This includes the title, subtitle, and author (must match verbiage on the book's cover).

Publisher Page: (required) On the back of the title page, this includes: publisher, copyright, ISBN, Library of Congress notice, publication information, legal notices, and year of printing. Credits for production, photography, editing, and illustration may also be included.

Dedication Page: (optional) Keep this short. Ideally, leave considerable white space on the page.

Acknowledgments Page: (optional) The author expresses gratitude for people who supported him and contributed to the book. Writers tend to overdo these, so readers don't read them. This can be combined with the dedication or placed in the back matter.

Epigraph: (optional) This is a short quote commonly used after chapter titles and before the text. One can also be placed on a blank left page, such as the one facing the table of contents.

Table of Contents: In nonfiction, list sections and chapters with enough detail to attract buyers and make it easy for readers to navigate the book. Use clever titles that have voice. Fiction books often don't have chapter titles.

Foreword: (optional) Written by someone other than the author and signed and dated, the foreword provides context for the book. Spell it correctly (not *foreward*, *forward*, or *forword*).

Preface: (optional) Written by the author, this tells how the book came about and provides details on production. This information can be included in the introduction.

THE BODY

Introduction: (optional) The author explains why the reader should read the book, places it in context, makes disclosures, and defines the book's scope and organization. If it is more than one or two pages, many readers won't read it. Be careful not to start the story in the introduction.

Prologue: (optional) Used most often in fiction, it sets the scene and is told from the point of view of a character or narrator. (Prologues are out of favor with some publishers.)

Section Breaks: (optional) Similar to acts of a play, a book can be divided into sections or parts. These begin on odd-numbered pages (the book's right-side pages).

Chapter Breaks: The first page of a chapter starts about one-third of the way down on an odd-numbered page (right-side page). In nonfiction, the chapter number, title, and epigraph (optional) are included. In fiction, only the chapter number is most commonly used. In historical writings, a date and place are often used as the chapter title.

Epilogue: (optional) A summation, in the voice of the author, character, or narrator, this is meant to tie up the ending by creating closure, bringing readers up to date, or to giving them satisfaction.

BACK MATTER (All Optional)

Appendix (or Addendum): Details and helpful tools

Index: Alphabetical list of words and associated page numbers

Glossary: Alphabetical list of terms and their definitions

Bibliography: Reference list of source information

Books by Author: List of books

About the Author: One-page or less biography

Starting a book is like driving down both sides of a road at the same time. Eventually, though, something sparks a thought that suggests the theme. For me, this means I'm centered, speeding, mastering curves, and getting my groove on while John Fogerty's "Centerfield" blasts, "Put me in, coach, I'm ready to play—today."

Chapter 11

BEGINNINGS

The honeymoon between author and reader lasts about three pages.—William Bernhardt

The beginning of the beginning is essential to a book's success. If you don't draw the reader in early on, you'll lose him, and it won't matter how wonderful the rest of the book is. Some readers may give a writer a break and continue for a few more pages, but agents, publishers, and contest judges won't. They will move on to more seasoned writers.

FIRST SENTENCE, PARAGRAPH, AND CHAPTER

Do not hoard what seems good for a later place in the book, or for another book; give it, give it all, give it now.—Annie Dillard

The beginning of a book has a lot of work to do. In fiction, main characters are introduced, as well as what they want and why they can't get it. Tension, conflict, curiosity, and intrigue are promoted. From whose point of view the story is being told is revealed. Time, place, and setting are established. Action, an inciting incident, or a defining moment are often used in the beginning to captivate and hint at the plot. In nonfiction, the premise and what the book offers readers is made clear and enticing.

When a potential buyer peruses a book, the buy or no-buy decision is most likely made after the first one or two paragraphs. Writers must create enough magic to immediately captivate readers. Nothing else matters if the beginning doesn't attract the intended audience.

First Sentence: The most important component of a book is the first sentence. It is so vital that most seasoned writers seek critique and rewrite it over and over, experimenting, and taking it to a higher level each time. A good first sentence is economical while being rich with detail and innuendo. It is wildly intriguing so that it grabs the reader and reels him in. A clever shock factor that creates intense curiosity delivers an exciting beginning.

The first sentence generally reveals the main character, his name, and indicates the point of view from which the story is being told. Starting with dialogue is controversial. Most experts say not to do so. I recommend avoiding any controversial craft issues early on in a book. Why take the chance of turning off an agent or a publisher with your first sentence?

Once the first sentence is mastered, make the first sentence of every chapter equally compelling. Examples at the end of this chapter illustrate first sentences, as well as second ones. Second sentences are crucial to explaining the first ones and in allowing them to be economical.

First Paragraph: This expands on the details presented in the first sentence by elaborating on the main character, hinting at the book's message, establishing time and place, describing the setting, creating curiosity, incorporating action, or at least hinting at action or high drama to come. Keep setting and character descriptions, as well as backstory, economical so they don't distract from the action, slow the pace of the story, or dwarf characters.

First Chapter: In most fiction, action—blazing, crazy, mind-blowing action—or intense drama of some sort are the great ways to draw in readers. The depth of information and more detailed descriptions are best introduced in subsequent chapters. Beginning with intense drama or where action happens usually requires an inciting incident or a defining moment of some sort. Consider an unconventional setting for this event.

Describe characters in more depth. Convey something intriguing about them, give them relationships, and reveal qualities that endear them to the reader. Divulge what the main characters want and the obstacles that keep them from getting it.

Incorporate drama or action and avoid anything that interrupts the forward flow of the story, such as long setting descriptions, backstory, or data dumps. Keep the reader in the moment. Focus on a brisk pace.

Introduce conflict and tension. Continue to generate curiosity. Divulge time and place and the cultural environment in which the drama or action takes place. Introduce just enough setting information to set the stage.

In both fiction and nonfiction, the first chapter often reveals, or at least hints at, the book's theme and primary message. It introduces a hook that is threaded throughout the book. These attributes keep readers reading.

In nonfiction, many forms of beginnings are available. Each category has its own proven formula for structure. For example, in essay, the premise is typically stated up front—clearly and factually. Don't allow structure formulas to stymie your creative spirit, though. If the mood strikes, get your crazy on and do the unusual.

SOMETHING DIFFERENT: Agents and publishers are looking for fresh ideas. If that is not delivered up front, a manuscript is rejected. Why? Because the peculiar is intriguing while the ordinary is trite and hard to sell. As John le Carré said, "The cat sat on the mat is not a story. The cat sat on the other cat's mat is a story."

- Expose something outrageous, odd, or eccentric in the first few pages. Include a shock factor.

- Have action happen in unusual or unlikely places.

- Introduce a comedic, bungling sidekick, a pet, or some other element of entertainment that causes readers to anticipate more of the same to come.

- In nonfiction, give readers fresh information and take concepts to a higher, more global level.

DON'T HOLD BACK: An author's most crucial and, sometimes, grueling writing decisions relate to what to put in and what to leave out. Don't hold back. Mike Duply said, "It's senseless to save that final twist, snazzy quote, or delicious tidbit until the end. . . . Instead, play your ace card first and sink your hooks into your reader."

Don't worry about running out of ideas. Include every literary notion you've got in your current work. An infinite supply of creative juices are in you. I've exhausted my Idea List several times. Each time, it blossoms again.

WHERE TO START A STORY

Start the story wherever the high-octane material begins.—Eliot Schrefer

Where to start a story depends on the genre. For many types of fiction, it's good to begin with an inciting incident or an action scene. In action-oriented genres, leave no doubt in the reader's mind but that some sort of action is coming, and hell is coming with it. In other genres, the beginning is a good place to promote mystery and curiosity. In his book, *The Crooked Letter,* Tom Franklin shows how one word—*monster*—can be incredibly effective at whipping up the fear factor in a crime mystery: "The Rutherford girl had been missing for eight days when Larry Ott returned home and found a monster waiting in his house."

The following fascinating nonfiction beginning about a 1930s event, written by Anne Barajas Harp, was published by This Land Press, Tulsa, Oklahoma, *Race Reader* in 2017.

The Trouble with Henry

Mary Popkess marched into the Sand Springs football stadium under a full head of steam. She made straight for the visitor's sideline where Homer

Hill was watching his undefeated Dewey Bulldoggers line up for kickoff in the 1938 Verdigris Valley playoffs. Hill, the wiry, electric coach one sportswriter tagged "The Real Little Napoleon of the Bench," had won 50 of his last 55 games and two conference titles. This night would be his third.

Popkess leaned into the coach. "They won't let Henry in," she said urgently over the noise of the crowd.

Hill walked to the line where players tensed for the whistle and pulled his team captain Carl Burget aside. Words were exchanged. Burget huddled with the other team seniors, leather helmets close together, then the rest of the players were gathered. Game officials were called in and more words were exchanged.

Minutes later, the officials and 4,000 eager football fans looked on in stunned bewilderment as the Dewey Bulldoggers walked off the field. They would understand why soon enough.

On paper, Henry was no one of particular importance—a deliveryman, a janitor, a colored man in a world that was starkly black and white. But he also was a man whose friendship and dignity inspired 30 boys to make an astounding act of loyalty.

Once you've hooked readers with a powerful beginning like this one, don't turn them loose. Reel them in.

****

EXAMPLES OF FIRST SENTENCES

First sentences have a lot of work to do, especially in fiction. They create curiosity, establish point of view, identify main characters, incorporate tension and conflict, hint at the theme, and seduce readers. I was asked to develop a list of first sentences as an exercise in a fiction workshop. It was great fun, so I share it below. You might practice by creating a list of your own.

Gage took what he wanted. Ellie knew, later, he would take more, and she would have to kill him.

Percy ignored the primal wailing from Wanda as he crammed Max's head into the barrel and considered shoving hers into it as well.

Mavis got pregnant trying to help Wally quit smoking, and that changed everything.

All three of Cecil's wives had died, and no one in Ada knew it—until the Internet happened.

The only good news Max had to offer Amanda after their wedding fiasco was that at least he didn't get blood on her dress.

Jason's mom killed his pet rat with a broom when he was five, and he didn't speak for two years.

Dixie, covered in blood, coolly proclaimed an excuse that made Officer Walt shudder, "I'm not a nice person."

Newbury, Iowa, was a town marinated in righteous Methodists who were not open to the invasion of an enthusiastic Southern Baptist like Val, a guy hell-bent on saving souls and bedding women.

After being gone for three years, Gus marched into Mandy's kitchen and checked the cabinet to see if the Jack Daniels was still there.

Colt walked in with a rakish swagger, looking better than any man ought to, and a brouhaha swirled and rumbled in Brandy's head.

Newt noted that some women got prettier as you got to know them, but Lucy, well, she just uglied up over time.

Mattie studied Jason as he meandered across the dance floor in her direction and concluded, *I would climb that tree.*

The company's medical director began to sweat when the owner's wife winked as she asked for oxycodone for fat ankles.

Sparky fidgeted so frantically as the cops approached that he looked like a disco dancer juiced up on meth.

Moose rode his motorcycle through a bunch of swarming bees one day, which explained the amputation.

I was drunk on a boat.

Note: Ordinarily, in a first sentence in a composition, an author would use the main character's first and last name since it's the first time the character is introduced.

EXAMPLES OF SECOND SENTENCES

A second sentence clarifies the first one, enhances its intrigue, and allows it to be economical. For example:

Jenny lay on the bathroom floor after throwing up, while Buck, in his pointy-toed, roach-killer boots, hovered in the doorway blocking out the hallway light. With both hands on the door jamb and leaning in, he asked, "Are you going to fix dinner?"

Brandy danced naked as the firemen packed up their equipment after freeing her toe from the bathtub faucet. Sheriff Hollister sweated.

Sheridan, exceptionally alluring in her vulnerable state, sobbed as Detective Conner interviewed her. The tattoo on her chest, *Audacious,* defied her victim status but unfortunately, Connor ignored that clue.

Pepper glared at Cody as she chased the pills with vodka and ripped her blouse open, popping off buttons and revealing shiny skin and bikini tan lines that would make any man want her. Cody froze.

Mandy was damaged, but she hid it well. Lucas, who saw through the mask, advised her that she wasn't depressed; she was just surrounded by assholes.

After their date, Bernice and her Vietnam vet boyfriend, high on pot, ate a whole box of Fruit Loops and the best raisins in the universe. She concluded this was a good time to kill him.

Wendy liked to think she accidentally found her boyfriends —just ran into them, like when you spot in-season cherries at the grocery store. The truth is, she hunted them down.

After spending ten years in the army, Cookie was trained to kill rather than fight, so she could stare down a mad pit bull. No one in his right mind would mess with her, but not everyone in Harvey's saloon was in his right mind.

Chance tended to gravitate toward irreverent, unrefined people. On a cruise, he had become bored with uppity, provincial, northeastern folks when, late one night, in the ship's nightclub, he heard a Texas woman yell, "Whiskey!"

Tanner was a linear man who, when confronted with an ink blot, a reclinable seat, or a dance position, saw something erotic. Then, he met Amanda, who operated brazenly with the enthusiasm of an Amazon woman warrior.

Wanda felt kidnapped when coupled up, and she wasn't one to fall in love with her kidnapper. The compulsion to rescue men from chicken-flavored ramen noodles was not in her repertoire.

Caiya, keeping his eye on the trappers in the boat, put the knife between his teeth and sank into the water. Unaware of the water moccasin at his feet, he pushed himself off the riverbank.

FAMOUS FIRST SENTENCES

"It is a truth universally acknowledged, that a single man in possession of a good fortune, must be in want of a wife."—Jane Austin, *Pride and Prejudice*

"It was a pleasure to burn."—Ray Bradbury, *Fahrenheit 451*

"I died three days ago."—William Bernhardt, *Capitol Offense*

"Once again," the man said, pulling the little girl along by the leash tied to his wrist and hers. "Tell me your name."—William Bernhardt, *Primary Justice*

"I was not sorry when my brother died."—Tsitsi Dangarembga, *Nervous Conditions*

"If I could tell you only one thing about my life it would be this: when I was seven years old the mailman ran over my head."—Brady Udall, *The Miracle Life of Edgar Mint*

"First I had to get his body into the boat."—Rhian Ellis, *After Life*

"They shoot the white girl first."—Toni Morrison, *Paradise*

"We went to the moon to have fun, but the moon turned out to completely suck."—M. T. Anderson, *Feed*

"Day One: My lady and I are being shut up in a tower for seven years."—Shannon Hale, *Book of a Thousand Days*

(Source: "William Bernhardt's Workshop Handout - 2018-2")

Being a good writer is 3% talent and 97% not being distracted by the Internet.—Anonymous

Chapter 12

THE IN-BETWEEN

When in doubt, have two guys come through the door with guns.—Raymond Chandler

It's a challenge to keep the in-between of a book from slumping, but it's imperative to do so. It is a good place for a writer to take a minor incident, embellish it, and turn it into a pièce de résistance. This is similar to the difference between humming while dusting and singing like an opera star.

In fiction and in story-like memoir, events, actions, and suspense are active. Defining moments change everything. The story deepens. Stakes are raised. Twists and turns surprise readers. Tension builds. Conflicts intensify. Characters evolve.

In nonfiction, especially in essay, information relates to a premise. Details are engrossing, intensely relevant, staunchly defended, and clearly and intelligently expressed and illustrated. Instructional and how-to pieces require specifics, clear directions, and detailed illustrations. And inspirational pieces call for plenty of emotive expressions. Children's books require strict adherence to requirements specifically established for various age groups.

Three key tactics that keep the middle vital and captivating are: (1) taking a tidbit—a minor incident—and embellishing it, (2) expertly blending narration, exposition, and dialogue, and (3) using an Idea List to add voice and to introduce humor. (Examples are presented at the end of this chapter.)

UNIVERSAL RELEVANCE: Turning a tidbit into a compelling story requires intense awareness. Orson Scott Card said, "Everybody walks past a thousand story ideas every day. The good writers are the ones who see five or six of them. Most people don't see any." To make incidents relatable to readers, make them more universal—communal. One of my poet friends calls this *going global*.

I described the following incident in my memoir, *Out of Iowa—Into Oklahoma*. The experience reflects a woman's tender vulnerability. The universal relevance of all women's fears were exploited with just three words "Every woman knew. . . ." It's good to go global.

My man left me for a much younger woman, which was devastating. At my nail appointment, I shared what happened with my manicurist. I cried and she cried. Soon the other manicurists around us and their customers became intrigued with the emotional turmoil. They got in on the story of betrayal and misery and teared up. It was a sad, sad, sorrowful situation.

Hairdressers became curious about the drama, and they and their customers were soon swept into the doom and gloom. Every woman knew in her soul it could happen to her, and a dark, angry cloud descended and swallowed us up as though the life force were being sucked out of us.

As we sank deeper and deeper into the abyss, our defenses included bashing the interloper, disparaging the unfaithful, and spewing man-hating dialogue, all of which further ravaged the anguished group. The cloud darkened, the gloom deepened, and happy salon chatter turned into melancholy whispers and awkward silence. The atmosphere was grim.

Later, sitting in my car as I left, I looked back inside the shop. A lady who had just entered looked around like, "What happened?" It was clear that, in spite of all the pretty hair and fingernails, I had single-handedly brought this normally cheerful, chatty, upbeat place down, down, down into the depths of despair. Dante couldn't have done it better.

Given the nature of my man's betrayal, I should have thought, *You aren't leaving, thank God, are you?* Instead, I felt like the victim of a drive-by shooting. And I shared that with everyone. I should have brought champagne and cake, but I brought Dante.

This was a defining moment that changed everything. Going forward, I still wrestled with the in-your-face demons of the loss and its aftermath, but I determined then and there I was going to save myself from the doom and gloom.

I couldn't do it, though. In spite of my resolve, I couldn't pull it off. The wound was too deep, the pain too intense, and that was the end of love as I knew it.

Human frailties are always interesting. Susan Glaspell said, "In writing . . . remember that the biggest stories are not written about wars, or about politics, or even murders. The biggest stories are written about things which draw human beings closer together."

TIDBIT EXERCISE: To convert a tidbit into something greater, put pen to paper and write whatever comes to mind about a topic or memory for at least fifteen minutes without stopping. All kinds of crap will come out, but jewels will pop out as well. Tap into them. After that, look beyond what was written for more global implications and create a story that is universally relevant. This requires going over and over the piece, layering on colorful details, embellishing content, expressing emotions, and ensuring what you write is germane to a broad spectrum of readers.

TRANSITIONS, FLOW, AND PACE

If you stumble over a sentence every time you review a document, that sentence needs work.

Once a story is fully developed, read the text aloud. Rewrite awkward phrases or sentences. Develop solid transitions from one sentence to another, one paragraph to another, and one chapter to another. End chapters on a dramatic note.

> **Hint:** To make a story a page-turner, put the resolution of an issue at the beginning of the next chapter.

To keep readers' attention throughout the middle, do a run-through and make certain every sentence is interesting in its own right—every single one. Never write something ordinary or tell the reader what he already knows. Weed out redundant sentences. Note anything common and make it more interesting. Make emotions deeper and more meaningful.

Don't limit the story to facts. Emphasize emotions and include sensory information. Dress up descriptions of people, settings, and circumstances. For example, instead of simply saying Oklahoma country boys were wilder than Iowa country boys in my memoir, *Out of Iowa—Into Oklahoma*, I said this:

> Oklahoma country boys are cowboys, who are like Iowa farm boys on speed. Dating one made me feel like a dog chasing a race car. I couldn't keep up. When he stopped, I didn't know what to do with him. That boy was everything I wanted and nothing I needed. Ultimately, he left me with my fire still burning. Turns out, that was a good thing.

Flow is vital to readability. For the most part, avoid long paragraphs and vary paragraph size. Interrupt narrative and exposition with dialogue, but make certain the dialogue is relevant and vital to the progression of the story. A wise writer goes through his piece, focused entirely on good order and smooth transitions, and then goes through it again to take out every unnecessary word. The "Run-Through Layering Process" in the Appendix speaks to these tasks.

PACE: Build up low spots. Up the stakes, increase the action, or introduce subplots. Surprise the reader—even shock him. Keep in mind, though, that continuous emotion or action exhausts the reader. Vary the intensity. Otherwise, the reader may feel as though he's been exposed to a Tasmanian devil. That can't be good.

As with music, mellow points make dynamic ones more effective. Apply intensity in waves. Ebb and flow. Spread out the action and intense scenes. Insert exposition, dialogue, and narration to slow things down. Make certain whatever you use is essential to the story.

NARRATION VERSUS EXPOSITION: *Narration* is the process of telling a story. *Exposition* explains or clarifies. These writing tools are often used interchangeably. Both are necessary, but they tend to slow the pace or to distance the reader from characters because they are *telling* as opposed to *showing*. Too much of either produces flat writing. Economically apply them and, for the most part, dole them out gradually in small doses. Nestle them between dialogue, drama, and action and, when using them, engage the reader through vivid imagery, impressive nouns, and powerful verbs.

UPPING THE STAKES

Ask yourself what could go wrong and write about that.—William Bernhardt

Readers love surprises. They also enjoy being tortured with hazards, perils, and the uncertainty of the unknown. Give them something to worry about. Change direction, up the stakes, have a character do the unexpected, the unachievable, or perhaps even the unacceptable.

I'm not one to read Westerns, but I read Larry McMurtry's *Lonesome Dove* twice because of the riveting twists and expertly developed characters. I cared about them, which made the surprises more impactful. Emotional connections between characters, as well as between characters and readers, keep a middle from slumping.

EMOTIONS—THE ULTIMATE STIMULI

For a reader to feel emotion, a character must experience it.

Emotional experiences connect characters and readers. Angela Ackerman and Becca Puglisi, authors of the book,

The Emotion Thesaurus, suggest that: "above all else, readers pick up a book to have an emotional experience. . . . [Readers] don't want to be told how a character feels; they want to experience the emotion for themselves."

Several indications of feelings or sensory reactions are appropriate for every scene. Be generous when inserting emotions into what you write. Without them, the middle slumps. Torture the reader. Scare him. Make him worry. Make him hurt. Make him cry. Then rescue him with exhilaration and hope as I did in this piece:

When we arrived home with my grandbaby, a morphine-induced state had his eyes glazed over. His stare tore at my insides. A sheen of sweat glowed on his face and neck as his tiny body fought to heal from wounds carved by a scalpel.

As I rocked and patted him gently, he transformed in my mind into something more than a baby. He became a creature of the universe, *a being* fighting to live. I wanted to will him to be well, to guarantee his future. I wished I could somehow transfer my life force to him, to make him whole.

Even with the intensity of those feelings, a peaceful contentedness prevailed within me. I felt gratefulness for his existence. Emotions welled up and took me over, their potency producing polite tears. Butterflies fluttered in my stomach as he settled on my chest—his weight pressing against me. I wondered how he could sleep so contentedly with all that stirring in my core.

Although salty tears made trails down my cheeks, a euphoric state took over as I held that vulnerable little soul fighting for his life. In that moment, I, the baby whisperer—a weeping, ordained, sixty-year-old warrior woman—felt fuller and more whole than ever in my life.

In fiction, emotions are generated through characters. In nonfiction, they come straight from the heart of the writer.

FLASHBACKS: Readers need to know enough about a character's history to care about him. Everyone has a past, which is relevant to the present. Flashbacks can reveal that history, but they need to be skillfully applied. Used improperly, backstory interrupts or slows the forward-moving action of a story. Stephen King said, "The most important things to remember about backstory are that (a) everyone has a history, and (b) most of it isn't very interesting." Some experts advise not using them in the earliest part of a book, particularly if they are long. History is usually best revealed in small doses or through dialogue rather than in long narratives. Make certain any flashback used is concise and relevant.

It's vital to masterfully transition into and out of a flashback. The reader needs to know when the timeframe changes. Use screen breaks if the flashback is very long. Otherwise, to transition into one, a writer can say something like, "He recalled the days when their relationship began." To transition out, he might say, "We had a chemistry back then that is missing now.

STAY THE COURSE

Flirt with quitting occasionally, but go back. Always go back. Don't die with your story still in you.

A major challenge of the *in-between* of a composition, which is about 60 percent of a work, is endurance. A writer knows that, to deliver, he must plant his ass in a chair and write hour after hour and day after day. He must have the patience to keep digging for more detail. He must engage in serious scene-building. He must embellish with sensory elements that enhance the story and keep the reader reading. But at times, a writer needs a break.

Take breaks. Take walks. Take a vacation. Paint something. Plant something. Cook something complicated. Listen to Michael Bublé or the Eagles. Drink Moscato and sniff essential oils. Get your freak on and ride a scooter—or not, per the advice of emergency room physicians.

As activity pumps blood to the brain, and the mind is distracted from pressure, creative thoughts come out of nowhere. They knock around in your head until you're compelled to go back to writing. Any doubts you had about the quality of that work in progress are quelled.

To rally, write something funny or shocking—or, better yet, something weird. And, in case you have ever experienced what you think is writer's block, consider this: author Terry Pratchett claims, "There's no such thing as writer's block. That was invented by people in California who couldn't write." I don't know about that. It's more likely that if you experience writer's block, it's because your meds are working.

****

EXAMPLES OF ENHANCING THE MIDDLE

These are Idea List items that were used during run-throughs to enhance the middle of my humorous prose compositions.

- Not being trendy, he thought Ariana Grande was a font.

- I sat captive in the plane's middle seat. The cultural attributes of my seat mates were reminiscent of those of Dumb and Dumber. I would have been better off sitting between a fretting baby and a marauding toddler.

- She claimed to be mechanically inclined, but the machines she could operate were limited to a stapler, a pencil sharpener, and a seatbelt (sometimes).

- His ADD kicked in—*one Mississippi, two Mississippi, three Mississippi, hokey pokey, marshmallows, polygamy, touchdown, unicorn, jigger of salt.*

- Our son's hippie college mates stopped by on their way to a peace and love event in Colorado. We gassed up their cars, packed vegetarian lunches, and searched for something for their dog. We didn't know if he was vegetarian, but we guessed not.

- It was not unusual for Donnie to go to the liquor store for breakfast. He was drunk when Camilla broke up with him, and she had to do it again the next day.

- Case put a message on the men's room wall to call Shelby for a mediocre time.

- Dating a younger man means dinner dates that include jalapeño poppers at Sonic followed by great sex on a futon. With an older man, you wake up in an AARP T-shirt.

- Pete worried the online test to discover the color of his aura would show he was plaid, or houndstooth or, worse yet, ecru.

EXAMPLES OF SHOCKING THE READER

These are the kind of twists that cause audiences or readers to gasp, laugh, go silent, pause, tear up, or go, "Wow!" or perhaps, "Geez." Do you have such moments in your story?

- Robert Redford gets shot in *The Natural*.

- Uhtred is sold into slavery in *The Lords of the North*.

- Captain Amazing gets accidentally killed in *Mystery Men*.

- The Red Wedding happens in *Game of Thrones*.

- Tony Perkins stabs Janet Leigh in a shower in *Psycho*.

- The main character's roommate is revealed as a hallucination in *A Beautiful Mind*.

- Gandalf falls into the abyss with the Balrog in *The Lord of the Rings*.

- Indiana Jones disarms a manic, sword-waving challenger by shooting him.

- Goose dies in *Top Gun*.

- An Irish lad dies from snake bites while crossing a river in *Lonesome Dove*.

If you're stuck, keep the faith, take a break, and then jump ahead and write the ending.

Chapter 13

ENDINGS

Great is the art of beginning, but greater is the art of ending.—Henry Wadsworth Longfellow

The process of writing the beginning or middle of a book might be a struggle, but the ending—wow—that's a Herculean challenge. And a writer must nail it or all is for naught. In a cringe-worthy statement, Truman Capote said, "Finishing a book is just like you took a child out in the back yard and shot it." That's typical Capote, who was known for excessive drama and a lack of sensitivity. Still, no writer would argue that endings are not monster challenges.

The end is all about climax and its aftermath—resolving conflicts, and tying up loose ends. Plots and subplots are tidied up. How characters have changed is demonstrated. It may take as many as ten efficient, intense scenes, urgently executed, to deliver a fast-paced, hard-hitting ending.

After the climax, readers are given closure through a satisfying resolution. A good ending pulls all the pieces in the plot, subplots, and relationships together and leaves no loose ends, unless they are intentional. A satisfactory ending to a story is not necessarily a Pollyanna one. Sad or shocking endings appeal to readers. After the movie *Saving Private Ryan* ended, audiences sat in their seats for some time, stunned and unable to move. At the end of *The Sixth Sense*, audiences gasped. At the end of *An Officer and a Gentleman*, the audience cheered. All three provoked emotional responses from viewers. A writer has done his job well when a reader puts a book down and is either pensive or he says, "Wow!"

CLIMAX AND RESOLUTION

When you think you're finished, add another layer—a punch.

A novel's climax and resolution is usually about five percent of the story and has a beginning, middle, and end, just as the global story does. It is dependent on everything the author created earlier, all melding into a conclusion. This can be played out in a number of scenes, each jutting in and out of the story and ramping up the tension just before the climatic release. This is accomplished through rising action (escalating conflict or a crisis) culminating in a peak point of tension, followed by falling action and resolution.

The ending might include hit after hit of action and a staccato release of information with a dark moment or confrontation before the satisfactory resolution. The peak point of tension, the climax, is the turning point that precipitates the release and the story's ending. It's most effective when the main character affects the outcome, whether that is vanquishing a villain, getting the girl, or resolving an issue.

After the climax, the main character's journey comes to an end and the point of that journey is revealed. He is transformed by the experience, and so are other characters. The story's theme and messages are wrapped up.

Hint: Once the ending has been determined, go back through the story and foreshadow—hint at—the ending without giving away the outcome.

In nonfiction, the ending draws conclusions and wraps up details. The premise is clarified; and the theme, reinforced. A salient—and often hopeful and inspirational—message is communicated.

After the ending is developed, you are not done yet. Take it to a higher level. Ask yourself how you can add punch or make it more universally relevant. And consider introducing a short, pithy last sentence—something memorable that sums up the story's message. End with a potent word or phrase.

READER SATISFACTION

No story is worthwhile to a reader
without a satisfactory conclusion.

The element of surprise in a climax is vital to meeting reader expectations. Nothing disappoints readers more than a clichéd ending. Deliver an out-of-the-ordinary one.

DÉNOUEMENT (dānoo'män): A post-climax wrap-up, the dénouement, deals with fallout from the climax, gives the reader satisfaction, and shows how characters have changed. It can suggest that characters are worthy of honor or redemption, or it can surprise the reader with some other twist that gives the reader closure. This often involves feel-good stuff, or it can endeavor to make sense out of tragedy. Give your readers satisfaction in the end.

****

WRITING CHECKLIST

If you cannot describe your book's ending as clever, perhaps even shocking, you are not done yet. Use the following writing checklist to promote great writing and to effectively build to a compelling ending.

———————————

_____Establish an overall narrative arc.

_____Map character arcs (characters should change over time).

_____Determine characters' internal and external qualities, including flaws and redeeming attributes.

_____Give the overall story and each chapter and scene a beginning, middle, and end.

_____Determine the book's premise and establish a theme.

_____Develop a plot and subplots.

_____Establish point of view (POV) for each scene/chapter.

_____Determine tense (past, present, future).

_____Determine person (first, second, third).

_____Write in active voice where appropriate.

_____Show, don't tell, where appropriate.

_____Transition smoothly from sentence to sentence, paragraph to paragraph, and chapter to chapter.

The Beginning:

_____Develop an off-the-charts, fascinating first sentence.

_____Consider an inciting incident, preferably action-packed.

_____Introduce main characters (protagonist, antagonist, supporting characters).

_____Give characters flaws, quirks, contradictions, talents, conflicts, and redeeming qualities.

_____Endear characters to readers.

_____Provide a sense of time, place, and setting.

_____Include a humorous, or otherwise captivating, sidekick.

_____Reveal what the main character wants and identify obstacles that keep him from getting it.

_____State or show why reader should care about the premise.

_____Create curiosity. Introduce conflict and tension.

The Middle:

_____Create a fabulous first sentence for every chapter.

_____Raise the stakes throughout.

_____Incorporate defining moments.

_____Include cliffhangers, teases, or a potent statement at the end of every chapter.

_____Foreshadow the ending without giving it away.

_____Include sensory elements and emotions in every scene.

_____Interject twists, turns, surprises, setbacks, and dark and hopeless moments. Intensify conflict.

_____Eliminate a character, or add one who changes things.

_____Vary pace and intensity; use narration or dialogue to lower intensity after a peak.

_____Embellish setting descriptions, character descriptions, and action descriptions (don't overdo).

_____Infuse tension into every scene. Make readers worry.

_____Recount dramatic events in a moment-by-moment fashion and in sharp detail.

_____Manage point of view.

The End:

_____Use multiple fast-track scenes to resolve plot/subplots.

_____Deliver a surprise twist. *Bam!*

_____Give information in staccato bursts—*rat-a-tat-tat!*

_____Show how characters have changed.

_____Tie up loose ends.

_____Give readers satisfaction through dénouement.

_____Develop an impactful last sentence.

If you choose to avoid the norm and follow eccentric instincts, write playfully so you don't end up the object of an intervention.

Chapter 14

WRITING WITH VOICE

Words perfectly nuanced and delivered in a cadence, well, there is just nothing else like that except, perhaps, the rare and efficient simile that hugs a reader in a way he will never forget.

As a writer, your most valuable commodity is your voice. It is key to avoiding blandness. I look at it this way: *You can call me inappropriate or offensive. You can call me unrefined or crude. You can call me ditsy or dopey. You can even call me weird. Just don't call me boring.* It's better to be a rogue writer than a timid one.

Seven agents and publishers serving on a panel at a San Francisco writers conference I attended were asked, "What is the most important quality you look for in a writer?" As panel members passed the microphone from one to another, each one responded, "Voice."

Readers may not understand the concept of voice, but when they experience it, they value it. Professor William Zinsser's book, *On Writing Well,* is used in journalism classes in universities around the world. It should be the cornerstone of every writer's library. In it, he said, "Your commodity is you. Don't alter your voice to fit your subject. Develop one voice that readers will recognize." Even when I write serious books, I cannot resist the temptation to add humor. That's part of my style and voice.

Voice is not an option. It is what sets a writer apart. If a book has no voice, the reader is like the person watching a boring movie who is hoping it will get better, but it never does. A moviegoer may not walk out of a bad movie, but a reader will, for sure, put down a boring book.

WHAT IS VOICE? It is the literary fingerprint of a writer. Voice delivers the zing through a symphony of words—quirky interpretations and robust revelations of the writer's impressions. Voice involves how a writer expresses emotions, delivers tone, and portrays action. When an author writes like no one else, his voice makes what he wrote memorable and valuable.

Voice involves distinctive expression through novel, potent words and syntax (the arrangement of words and phrases). It is about speech patterns that give what is written personality. It means a writer is unique, witty, sarcastic, inspirational, and inventive. Voice is seductive. It draws readers in and holds them. And it impresses publishers.

A writer's ability to write with a unique voice is a matter of craft. It requires he muster the courage to break rules and to say and do things that are expressive and unusual. This means he must be loud and intriguing enough to go beyond the noise in the literary world—to stand out in the swarm of writers. Be resolute about inserting your voice into your writing so it is different from anyone else's.

Turning your crazy, mad, flamboyant self loose requires that you buck up and be bold. George Carlin described how he found his voice in comedy, after which his career took off. He learned to distinguish himself from other comedians by not holding back—by being himself. He said things no one else would say. It took guts to spew a lyrical list of swear words on television, accompanied by wildly quirky facial expressions, especially in the 1970s. And it worked.

Some say voice is innate—you either have it or you don't. Not true. Voice is not necessarily something that happens to a writer. It is something he can consciously develop. Cultivate voice and express yourself in unique, personal ways. Here's how.

LAYERING—THE KEY TO FINDING VOICE

Your voice will come from revision.

Voice may come naturally to some, but anyone can cultivate their own way of expressing themselves. What is required to do so is courage, imagination, and revision.

Gordon A. Kessler said, in his book, *Story Masters,* "Much of your voice will come through editing, revising, and rewriting." Constance Hale, in her book, *Sin and Syntax,* said, "Voice involves more than following the simplistic command of 'Write the way you talk' . . . [It involves] painstaking revision."

As I've said before, if going over a draft multiple times bothers you, remember that *revision is writing*. It is the nature of the writing process. It is why authors often take years to write a book.

To find your voice, begin by researching *writing with voice* online and by studying it through books and workshops. Every book on writing talks about voice.

177

While doing all that learning, apply revision processes to your compositions.

Two effective tools I apply during revision to facilitate the introduction of voice are:

- The Run-Through Layering Process

- An Idea List

(These are illustrated at the end of this chapter and in the Appendix.)

FINDING VOICE THROUGH LAYERING: This process yields significant enhancement opportunities. It involves doing a run-through of a book, focused entirely on finding voice and taking the writing to a higher level. This can take several months, but it is time well spent. It is a writer's investment in himself.

The suggested topics for run-throughs listed in the Appendix include one on voice. As you apply this layering process to develop your own voice—go page by page, paragraph by paragraph, through your document. Do not leave a page until voice is in there. Tell your audience what they don't already know and deliver it in a way they've never before experienced. Embellish. Surprise them.

The goal of a voice run-through is to make each page fascinating, compelling, intriguing, entertaining, vivid, frightening, comforting, inspirational, informative, or more interesting. Don't go to the next page until the current one has at least one of these attributes. After this process, your composition will speak loudly. It will sparkle.

When writing fiction, the author's voice should never overtake the voice of a character. Know your characters well and speak from their perspectives. Give them voices. Develop main characters with voices so distinctive that readers know who is speaking without you telling them. And never let your voice as the author take the reader out of a story.

In most nonfiction, these restraints don't apply. An author's voice is free to reign supreme.

Be audacious about putting yourself into what you write. This is what makes what you produce valuable. Each run-through of a draft introduces another layer of polish. The manuscript will show so much improvement each time that you'll be grateful you did it one more time. For this reason, run-throughs are addictive. You will want to do them again and again, and after each one, you'll thank yourself for doing it. This process is enabled by the use of an Idea List.

FINDING VOICE IN AN IDEA LIST: This resource, described in Chapter 3 on "Craft," is essential to cultivating voice. It sparks creative notions. In a sense, an Idea List serves as a writer's imagination.

> **Hint:** Since my Idea List includes my own ideas and those of others, I underline anything that is a direct quote from any source that might require an attribution.

Here are examples of jewels I've collected in my forty-some-page, computerized Idea List:

- I'm so happy, I could just wash dishes.

- Balance: A person can do too much or too little of anything. (This is close to a universal truth.)

- Just by being, you are enough.

- He suffered the inconvenience of being a feminist.

- She is so elegant in her weirdness.

- I'm in a Bee Gees frame of mind.

- Cowboys often do not play well with others.

- <u>You are braver than you believe, stronger than you seem, and smarter than you think.</u>—Christopher Robin

I also collect words and phrases in my Idea List. Wonderful expressions, such as these treasures: chutzpah, primal, regal, grief bacon, the epitome of stupid, the medicine is mine, rusty love, in lieu of tasing, cushioned with foliage, big girl stretch pants, so-o-o pedestrian, audacious narcissism, <u>sit in a cloud</u>, wicked old, verbal dexterity, stupid wonderful, and karmic doozy (payback).

If you don't have an Idea List of some sort, start one.

Application of the Run-Through Layering Process and using an Idea List are illustrated in the following Dedication from my memoir-esque book about aging, *Near Sex Experiences—A Woman in Crescendo, Aging with Bravado.* The first draft in these examples was uninteresting. After a voice run-through using notes from my Idea List, the dedications came to life:

First Draft: Dedicated to Sam Elliott, a fabulous older man whom I have adored for years.

With Voice: Dedicated to Sam Elliott, a fabulous seventy-one-year-old masculine piece of bravado and sensitivity who enters a scene with a rakish swagger, causing the air around him to dissipate as he holds the universe together.

First Draft: Dedicated to the men I've loved.

With Voice: Dedicated to the men I've loved. Because of them, when I'm asked to check a box for sex on forms, I draw my own box for *not pertinent*.

First Draft: Dedicated to my friends—my tribe—who soften my world and give me advice and counsel.

With Voice: To my mixed salad of friends—my tribe—who soften my world and offer up symphonies of advice. Although always issued with love, this advice is sometimes misguided. After a complicated romantic breakup, one of my tribe advised that if I wanted to get stalked, I should go to a furniture store or a car lot.

First Draft: Dedicated to my therapist, who saved me at a critical time.

With Voice: Dedicated to my therapist who, when I mucked around in a funk and bared my soul, had the self-discipline not to say, "Well, that was weird."

The voice in these dedications reveals the writing style, sets the tone of the book, and introduces the genre—humorous prose. And it is directed at a clearly defined target audience—women over fifty.

The wit suggests readers can expect more humor, and it entices them to read on. (It might also suggest the introduction of a new genre—old-adult fantasy.) The uniqueness of these dedications surprises the reader. No one would describe them as boring. After reading the first dedication to Sam, readers are likely to read the rest of them (dedications are often skipped)—as well as the book.

SPECIFICITY OF DETAIL: Concrete detail appeals to the senses and enhances voice. Consider the difference between the following alternatives:

- *Dad had to have brain surgery.*

- *In a six-hour surgery, a surgeon cut two small, but deadly, tumors from the base of Dad's skull.*

A run-through where you review each sentence and consider how to make it richer yields opportunities like this one. Don't overdo, though. Pick just the right moments to enhance and sharpen what you communicate.

TONE: Books have attitude. Tone reflects that attitude. It's atmospheric and intermingled throughout the text. The expression of emotions delivers tone. These emotions can be blatant or discreet, consciously developed or organically evolved. Either way, they reflect the writer's perspective and his voice.

An astute writer is aware of the tone he is producing because he defines it up front and intentionally delivers it. As you express voice, be mindful of the resulting tone so it doesn't contradict your message. Defining your approach to a composition and its message provides guideposts and boundaries that ensure delivery of the desired tone.

Tone is significantly influenced by genre. A mystery or a thriller will have a different tone than an inspirational piece or a romance. It is generally best not to stray too far from the tone readers of each genre expect. However, unexpected humor is almost always appreciated. In a serious business document, the following broke up the soberness nicely and softened the tone:

> In a job interview, an interviewer asked, "What is your greatest weakness?"

> The applicant responded, "I'm too honest."

> "That doesn't seem like a weakness."

> "I don't give a crap what you think."

TESTING FOR VOICE: In his book, *Writing Tools: 55 Essential Strategies for Every Writer*, Roy Peter Clark said, ". . .the most powerful tool on your workbench to test your writing voice is oral reading." Read your story aloud, to test for voice. Read slowly and deliberately, as if you were reading to an audience.

GET YOUR SWAG ON: In respect to voice, being a rogue writer is better than being a careful one. Traction to be gained from fearless expression of voice is profound. Maya Angelou said, "If you are always trying to be normal, you will never know how amazing you can be." Express yourself in clever ways so your writing is distinguishable from every other writer. You will know you've mastered voice when you don't write like anyone else.

Explore the unique, fascinating meanderings going on in your head. Show them off with panache. Once voice is mastered, shipping a manuscript off to an editor feels good because you know it is authentic and uniquely yours. This is a feeling similar to that experienced when you are in a dental chair, the gas takes hold, and ABBA's song, "Dancing Queen," comes through the earphones.

****

EXAMPLES OF LAYERING VOICE

The following examples demonstrate how the "Run-Through Layering Process" (described in the Appendix) and an Idea List facilitate the infusion of voice. The underlined words were sourced from my Idea List during revision. They illustrate the value of such a list and the revision process.

First Draft: Travis could never top Dixie. She always got the better of him.

With Voice: Travis could never top Dixie. She tossed off verbal hand grenades like they were marbles rolling off a table. He came home from a hunt, boasting about bagging a buck. Using her swollen belly like a howitzer, she said, "Yeah, well, I made a kidney."

First Draft: Readers need a break from high intensity.

With Voice: Readers need a break from high intensity. Otherwise, they feel as if they're handcuffed to Kevin Hart.

First Draft: Writing mechanics include the process of formatting, which is tedious and boring.

With Voice: When it comes to formatting, I ask myself, "My life has come to this?" It's not a fanciful task. I take no pride in it, and I know I won't find my happy there. But it must be mastered, and rather than lounging around in self-pity, I tell myself it's better than diabetes.

First Draft: Blake's girlfriend's disposition was so erratic, it almost got him killed.

With Voice: Blake's <u>hellcat</u> girlfriend, Ruby, introduced an <u>emotional terrain</u> that darted around like a <u>laser light</u> and almost got him killed.

First Draft: Sheridan sobbed in the interview, so Conner hired her.

With Voice: Sheridan sobbed in the interview, so Connor hired her, not that the leather skirt and <u>handcuffs</u> hanging from her <u>studded belt</u> had anything to do with his decision.

First Draft: Writers call this "killing your darlings."

With Voice: Writers call this "killing your darlings," those precious, eloquent creations that make you feel as though you are on the verge of a <u>Shakespearean experience</u>.

First Draft: Author Brent van Staalduinen recommends starting stories at a point where it's too late for the characters to turn back.

With Voice: Author Brent van Staalduinen recommends starting a story at a point where it's too late for the characters to turn back: someone got drafted, got pregnant, got a DUI, got a psycho roommate, wrecked a relationship, hit a pedestrian, married the wrong person, won in Vegas, lost in Vegas, <u>got so drunk he changed the wrong flat tire</u>, or <u>got so high he sat at a stop sign waiting for it to turn green</u>.

Writing that is lush with stylistic overkill may be fascinating in an Andy Kaufman kind of way, but it's overwhelming. When I read heavy styling, it makes me feel like I do when helping a grandchild with homework on a computer, and I realize I don't know what a browser is.

Chapter 15

WRITING WITH STYLE

A good style should show no signs of effort. What is written should seem a happy accident.—W. Somerset Maugham

The difference between voice and style is subtle. Voice is about *what* a writer says—his message, impressions, and interpretations. It reflects a writer's personality through emotions, actions, descriptions, and other content. Style is broader and involves *how* voice is communicated. It's similar to the medium with which an artist paints a picture —the canvas, the paints, the strokes—as opposed to the details of the picture itself.

Style can be ornate, complex, comprehensive, wordy, packed with imagery, and rich with metaphors. Or it can be sparse, simple, efficient, and conversational. A style can be heavily researched, academic, formal, and authoritative like David Grann's *Killers of the Flower Moon* or Jane Mayer's *Dark Money*. Or it can be casual, dark, and witty like David Sedaris in *Let's Explore Diabetes with Owls*. Then there is the style of Dr. Denis Leary, who is known for stacking adjectives and talking smack as he did in *Why We Suck*.

One writer's style shows a preference for short, choppy sentences and short paragraphs while another's is rich with narration, complex sentences, and long paragraphs like Virginia Wolf's writing. Hemingway's short bursts and Stephen King's straightforward prose are recognizable from just a few paragraphs because their styles are so well developed.

Style can be too obvious. Richard A. Lanham says, "The best style is the never-noticed." A writer can do too little or too much of anything. Balance is vital. A good writer walks a fine line between impressive style and distracting excesses. However, excesses work for some writers. With a certain *je ne sais quoi*, some writers make a career out of indulgent word extravaganzas that critics would label overkill. Be brave and consciously develop a personal style. Make it one you're comfortable with while still appealing to readers. Personally, when it comes to style, I'd rather land in the outlandish arena than to be accused of being dull.

LAYERING STYLE

Style is shaped through revision.

Like voice, style evolves as compositions are written over and over. For some writers, style is innate, and it comes easily. Others must dig deep to find it. First drafts are rarely lush with style, although, for some people, the free-flow method of developing a draft promotes a naturally evolving style—sometimes an excess of it. Yes, a writer can demonstrate too much style. This is identifiable when a style is so impressive it interferes with the message or takes on the appearance of showing off.

Using the run-through layering technique during revision delivers style, just as it does voice. Remember, style is *how* you write, not so much *what* you write. Be brazen about cultivating the *how*.

STYLE AND TITLES: Establish your style early on through clever, informative titles:

- A poem titled *Mom* could be *I've Been Mom-ed.*

- A serious essay titled *On Aging* could be *The Inconvenience of Being Old.*

- An opinion piece titled *Consumerism* could be *The Drug of Consumerism.*

- A story titled *Eating Disorders* could be titled *An Adversarial Relationship with Donuts.*

A compelling title attracts an audience and tells readers what a book is about. A subtitle elaborates on the title and suggests what a book offers readers. Titles are vital marketing tools. Pack everything into them you can. Produce book and chapter titles that shout, "You need to read this!" Great titles, unexpected and lush with voice and style, jazz up a table of contents and help sell a book. Examples of such titles are listed at the end of this chapter.

SPOTLIGHTS: This stylistic technique uses short, choppy sentences to surprises readers. Spotlights are especially potent when placed between longer sentences or at the end of chapters. They involve making observations in clever, crisp ways. The staccato effect of a spotlight adds drama and voice.

- It freed his freak.

- I'm not obsessive.

- He's girl stuck.

- Fashionistas don't write.

- The dog is an anti-pet.

- Mom went gangster on him.

- I didn't mean that weird-like.

THE POWER OF NAMES: Because names influence how readers visualize characters, they foreshadow roles and behaviors. They also influence the ambiance of a book and enhance its style. Names insinuate a character's culture, age, disposition, and personality. Pick impressive names and use them to define characters. Here are examples.

- A country girl is Dallas; a peppy city girl, Poppy. A sweet girl is Meadow; and a sassy gal, Pepper. A mature woman is Hazel, Mable, Effie, or Lulabelle.

- A gas station mechanic is Ode. A good ol' boy is Tank.

- A distinctive man is Maxwell, Mason, Fillmore, or Noble; a shyster, Sturgill. A cowboy is Rowdy; an old cowboy, Angus.

- A determined detective is Hawk or Deacon. A male love interest is Slade, Cade, Gage, or Tanner.

- A doofus is nicknamed Goose or Morty. A hapless, comedic guy is Scooter. An upbeat jokester is Sparky.

- A Generation X-er is Heather, Bryan, or Jason.

- A hyped-up dog is Tango; a sophisticated dog, Barkley. A silly dog is Knuckles; and a hound dog, Drool. GiGi is a yappy, feisty little thing; and Thunder, a beast.

- An old car is named Betsy or Stanley. A new one is Roxie or Dash. An unreliable one is Sassy.

Names are rich with innuendo, and they are fun and potent. A writer misses a rare and profound opportunity if he names a character Steve or Sarah. Use an ordinary name only when it's important to suggest a staid, bland personality. Use names appropriate for the genre. Uncle Skillet, his brother, Bucket, and Aunt Weezie clearly suggest a comedic piece. Truman and Ernestine imply a serious one.

Starting more than one character's name with the same letter can be confusing to readers. Avoid using first and last names together after initially introducing a character's full name. Pick either the first or last name, or a nickname, and use it throughout the piece.

EXPLOITING WORDS
TO CREATE STYLE

Collect words with the passion of an art collector. Write them down. Own them. Manipulate them and apply them in unusual ways. Words are everything to a writer.

Using words in unusual ways is a matter of style. Like with voice, an Idea List facilitates making style happen. From such a list, I selected o*verachieving* to describe a bushy beard and *eccentric* to describe a pickup truck and a piece of furniture. *Feral* defined spring breakers in Florida as *the feral children* and lost love as *love turned feral.*

I've made up words like *undersmart, happy-ish,* and *Garbo-esque,* as well as the word combinations *micro ambitious* (for a go-getter), and *macro ambitious* (for a slacker). Grandchildren were named *Thing 1* and *Thing 2,* and two little girls, *The Sparkles.* An ex was described as burdened with *audacious narcissism.* A mooning incident was described as a *near-sex experience* (which ended up as the title of a book).

Look for bland words and replace them with more interesting and uniquely descriptive ones—not bigger, more impressive ones, but better ones. For example:

- Instead of *find out*, say *discover, explore*, or *fathom*.

- Instead of *home*, say *hovel, cottage, mansion*, or *pad*.

- Instead of *little*, say *petite, lithe, willowy*, or *elfin*.

- Instead of *big*, say *Amazonian, massive*, or *towering*.

- Instead of *bad hair*, say *a savage hairdo*, or *hair like a fishing lure* or *cotton candy*.

- Instead of *important*, say *critical, crucial, essential, consequential, significant*, or *notable*.

Using words in an atypical way, especially when describing sensual qualities, can deliver clever and memorable results. I used the word *leather* in a novel way to describe the sense of smell in the following example:

Cowboys smell like leather. It's a subtle aroma unless they are wet or gathered en masse, at which point the odor becomes pungent with musky attributes. At times, cattlemen smell like a blend of leather, cow shit, hay, and horse hair. That's not attractive, but with rough hands, tanned faces, sturdy demeanors, well-worn boots, and Wranglers fitted just so, the appeal remains.

That description was born when a group of eight cowboys came into a restaurant after braving a rainstorm. If I had not made note of the smell and put that note in my Idea

List, this unique and personal interpretation of cowboys would have, no doubt, been lost forever.

STYLE AND WRITING WELL

Magnificent style embodies a kind of audacious swagger, like that of a nattily attired Fred Astaire.

Quality writing is essential to demonstrating great style. You don't want your style to be interpreted as sloppy, amateur, or dull. Writing well is so fundamental that William Zinsser wrote a book, *On Writing Well*, and Stephen King wrote one, *On Writing*. Serious writers will take their advice, study writing craft and aspire to write well.

BE A READER: Observe other writers' styles. Note what makes their writing stand out as unique and personal. Contemplate what qualities of style work for you and what do not. And use the processes in the Appendix. They will help you develop your own style.

Craft is mostly well-defined. Style, on the other hand, is more nebulous and individual. And it is most effective when it's a nuanced result.

A writer is obliged to walk a line between expressing himself in interesting and entertaining ways while showing no effort. He must also balance conformance with breaking rules. When he does vary from established writing principles and practices, it needs to be in the interest of creativity, entertainment, or getting a point across.

Both voice and style come with the mandate to be different. This means a writer demonstrating authorship is both creative and gutsy. Express your voice and style with the aplomb of a rebel and the finesse of an expert.

THE PROMISE OF STYLE

People want to know why I do this, why I write such gross stuff. I tell them I have the heart of a small boy . . . and I keep it in a jar on my desk.—Stephen King

Triteness is a fatal flaw—a crime against literature. The key to avoiding it is to develop your own style and to express it blatantly. Let the creative juices flow and write in your own unique way. It takes courage to do that and to fling your work out into the world because, in doing so, you open yourself up to criticism. Don't let anyone's judgment rob you of self-expression. Be bold. Write whatever you want, and write it any way you want.

If you don't deliver a professional composition that is uniquely yours, you fail to honor your implied promise of a worthwhile product. Don't disappoint. Demonstrate courage squared, and deliver something uncommon that is notably yours and worthy of your readers' time.

A critic once told me my book on writing was too aggressive. In it, my advice to writers was candid, direct, and somewhat at odds with industry perspectives. I held my position because there were writers who needed the dose of reality my message delivered. And no one else was giving it to them. Many have thanked me. If I had perpetuated unfortunate writer issues, rather than examining them and proposing fresh perspectives, I might as well not have written the book.

Find your sweet spot in the writing world and express yourself fiercely. Create the gift of writing only you can give. Be an unapologetic scribe who speaks his truth. Be that person—the one with style.

****

CHAPTER TITLES
WITH VOICE AND STYLE

The following chapter titles from my memoir, *Red Heels and Smokin'—How I Got My Moxie Back,* reflect voice, style, and tone. They also hint at the theme.

DON'T DATE STUPID (PUN INTENDED) - Love Can Be Annoying

ONLINE DATING MADNESS - People Who Lie on the Internet Complain That People Lie on the Internet

REDNECK MACHO SHITHEADS* - There Ain't No Way You Can Love Him More than His Dog or His Horse Does

LOST CONNECTIONS - Prowling—It Rained Men, Until It Didn't

WRT (WOMAN RIGHT THERE) - Men in Packs at Work

TECHNOLOGY SPANKED ME - Kicking and Screaming into the Digital Age

THE AGING FAIRY BITCH-SLAPPED ME—HARD - My Personal Trainer Tried to Kill Me

PERHAPS I LOOK BETTER FROM THE BACK - How to Have Game—or Not

SOMETIMES I DO THINGS I SHOULDN'T - My Children Say, "Don't Call Me If You Get Thrown in Jail."

INVISIBLE—AT SIXTY, YOU BEGIN TO DISAPPEAR - The Sting of Dismissiveness

RELEVANCE: GETTING MY MOXIE BACK - Refusing to Disappear

---

*I use this label lovingly and have learned that any man who fits into this category is proud of it.

You know you had a good time when the next morning you find glitter in your bellybutton and your toothpaste won't foam.

Chapter 16

WRITING WITH HUMOR

Bump and grind music blasted. Lights flashed with a vengeance. Women were going nuts. Savanna lifted her head from staring at the napkin on which she calculated the club's profit that night. She glanced at the gyrating stripper and said to her frenzied girlfriends, "I'm going on record here. I don't like the guy's shoes."

An effective way to add voice and express unique style is through humor. Even a serious book can benefit from a dash of comedic effect. The more unexpected the humor, the more profound its impact. Consider how characters in movies grab audiences. Both the hero and villain in *Die Hard* throw out comedic surprises. And who can forget Ouiser's (pronounced *Weezer)* line in *Steel Magnolias*: "I'm not crazy. I've just been in a really bad mood for forty years." Humor is potent.

Don't be afraid to use humor in nonfiction. Even William Zinsser, a serious, scholarly writer, advised, "If something strikes me as funny in the act of writing, I throw it in just to amuse myself." And Niki Porter, senior editor of *The Writer* magazine, said, "Never be ashamed for wanting to write fun fiction or nonfiction. It isn't junk. It's necessary. And anyone who tries to shame you for it should be tossed from your life like the rubbish they are."

Wow! Tell us what you really think, Niki. She's right, though. Don't be intimidated by what uptight folks think—unless those people are your audience. Instead, consider the influences of comedic writers Tom Robbins and Dave Barry. Or, depending on your audience, your humor might take on a sarcastic, edgy tone. Either way, because it's fresh, humor provides an opportunity to express voice and to influence style.

Even something as serious as grammar rules can be targets for humor. Some requirements are ridiculously complicated. I apply humor to language rules in my workshops as illustrated below. This educates—somewhat —while entertaining an audience on a serious topic.

GRAMMAR NONSENSE

Grammar will make your head hurt. For example, following is the answer given on a grammar Internet site to the burning question: "What is the difference between past perfect and past participle?"

Past perfect combines "had" with the past participle of the verb. The past perfect is similar to the present perfect because the event also started in the past. However, the difference between the events is that the past perfect event also ended in the past.

Let me simplify this. If you use *had* frequently in your writing, reconsider the tense in which you write.

Another example of confusing grammar criteria is verb conjugation. The rules that govern this are baffling. One Internet explanation of this rule is:

> *"Would" is a past tense form of "will." It is also a conditional verb that indicates an action that would happen under certain conditions, which fits under the umbrella of the concept of verb conjugation. Some verbs are irregular and both regular and irregular verbs have obscure tenses.*

I have no idea what this grammatical mumbo jumbo means, and nothing I've read or done has brought clarification. So let me simplify this explanation. If you use *would* frequently in your writing, reconsider the tense in which you write. Instead of saying, "Mom *would* make pot roast on Sundays," say, "Mom made pot roast on Sundays."

Other tense matters involve *past progressive tense* and *transitional verbs*. When I discovered these, a brouhaha swirled and banged around in my head, and I accepted that I was befuddled, a common condition caused by grammar, third-grade math, and my Apple watch. Then, there is the issue of split infinitives, which—since *Star Trek* used the phrase "to boldly go"—no one gives a crap about anymore, except serious grammarians, whom younger generations avoid. I'm with them. I'm old but trendy—like, I no longer have a landline.

When grammar makes your head hurt, take an aspirin, watch crazy cat videos, drunk-cut your bangs, upholster a recliner, or get busy analyzing the geophysical metrics of angles and quadrants. And, if for any reason you think I present the above information to show off, know that I am admittedly undersmart (my new favorite word). I am wise in some respects, though. I know that, if you use *had* and *would* too often, you appear amateurish. You're welcome.

LAYERING COMEDIC EFFECTS

Humorous writing is the universe strutting its stuff.

Comedic effect is appropriate in any genre, no matter how serious the topic. To introduce humor, apply the same process of repeated revision used to add voice and style. Do a run-though. Mine your Idea List. Become an expert at taking your observations and the words of others and putting your own comedic spin on them. Here are techniques for incorporating humor into writing.

SELF-DEPRECATION: George Gobel said, "Did you ever get the feeling the world was a tuxedo and you were a pair of brown shoes?" This illustrates a classic comedy technique—deprecation, a literary weapon.

EMBELLISHMENT: Comedic writing thrives on this, but you must strike a balance between truth and exaggeration.

THOUGHT SHOTS: These are the character or a narrator's internal, colorful thoughts within a story, usually expressed in italics. When presenting thoughts, avoid using "he (or she) thought" to introduce them when you can. The reader will interpret words as thoughts from the italics

Thought shots reveal the personality of the person having the thoughts, while conveying vital, punchy, and often humorous information. They are so powerful that a writer should not include too many or take the reader out of the story with one. To be effective, thoughts must be relevant, fascinating, and uncommon. For example:

- *I'll wear leather so I smell like a new truck.*

- *Her regal, narcissistic nature was irritating. I should have brought her a gift—a fabulous picture of me in a lovely frame.*

- *This place is tacky in a Herculon upholstery kind of way.*

- *When did I become the asshole whisperer?*

ZINGERS: These involve using humorous phrases in unexpected places, particularly when surrounded by serious narrative. This works particularly well when a zinger is the last phrase in a series:

- He exercised poor judgment, demonstrated limited verbal dexterity, and looked like he had gotten drunk and dressed.

- I romanticize about the unattainable—pirates, robots, and Gene Hackman.

REPEATS: This is best described through examples: Kramer entering the room on *Seinfeld* or Norm's greeting in *Cheers* and the customers' responses.

TRANSITIONS: Humor at the end of chapters encourages people to read on. The end of a chapter in my memoir, *Near Sex Experiences*, illustrates that:

I no longer looked at a handsome man and thought, *I want some of that*. Instead, I felt like a cat about to be hit by a car. However, love is an opiate, and it smoldered. Flow with me here. Things got worse.

EMOTIONS: Humor is most effective when emotions are involved. The reader should care about the comedic character. Orson Scott Card said, "The Three Stooges and the Marx Brothers made people laugh, but they never really made people care." Make your readers care.

CREATING COMICAL CHARACTERS

Describe someone in colorful clothes as looking like three-quarters of a donkey cart. Or label her a piñata and threaten to beat her with a stick.

Humor is universal. Even serious books can benefit from quirky, bungling characters or smart alecks who add a dash of sarcasm. Doc Holliday's sarcastic comment to an adversary during a tension-filled scene in *Tombstone* is classic: "You know, Ed, if I thought you weren't my friend, I just don't think I could bear it." Occasionally, portray villains and serious characters as comedic. The more right and proper they are, and the more traditional their persona, the more effective the humor when delivered through their dialogue or actions. Such humor surprises readers, which adds to its impact.

An out-of-character comedic reaction is a joy to behold. Who can forget the scene in *Fried Green Tomatoes* when the ordinarily accommodating, passive Evelyn Coach, played by Kathy Bates, responded to the mouthy girls who stole her parking place. The girls justified their action by bragging that they were younger and quicker. Evelyn rammed their car—three times, no less—and announced, "Face it, girls, I'm older, and I have more insurance." The movie audience cheered.

Rather than say a character is funny, or anything else for that matter, show it. Make her humorous through what she says and does, what others say about her, or what happens to her. Instead of describing a person as sensitive, say, "She believes the purpose of bread is to feed ducks." Or "She doesn't fish because of an uncontrollable urge to rescue bait." Or, better yet, reveal her sensitivity through action or dialogue.

A CONTRACT WITH READERS

An author owes his readers what only he can give.

As professionals, writers have an implied contract with readers to deliver something special that is worthy of their time. By not writing in fresh, captivating ways, writers fail to honor that commitment.

While this implied contract inspires a writer to put his work out there, in reality, a writer's willingness to endure the torture of the writing process is more likely determined by his DNA (what he was born to do). Otherwise, he wouldn't do it, particularly if he's not making money, his work is not broadly distributed, and accolades are sparse. Still, he writes.

A writer vacillates between concluding his writing is trash and deciding it is brilliant. During times of splendor, he knows why he writes. Those moments trump the unnerving challenges every writer faces. To create your moments of splendor, be a flagrant, joyful, unapologetic scribe, one who tantalizes his readers. Grab them, pull them in, speak with a powerful, unique voice, and, make them laugh. Always make them laugh. Be that person.

****

EXAMPLES OF LAYERING HUMOR

The Run-Through Layering Process was used to introduce comedic effects into the following examples:

- I told my doctor that Trans-Vaginal Ultrasound seemed like a good name for a rock band.

- No doubt, Ouiser from *Steel Magnolias* could take out *Saturday Night Live's* church lady . . . if there were mud.

- A grape escaped the bunch, rolled off the counter, bounced, and meandered across the kitchen floor, as Rachael yelled, "Run! Run! You're free! You're free!" It is now a raisin.

- Ralph is a go-getter. He takes his wife to work, and then he goes and gets her.

- Vickie, a California sophisticate, womansplained to Stan, who was fresh in from St. Louis and newly divorced, "If you intend to date here, you need to get a better watch."

- On their first date, Cooper took Babs to a cock fight, after which, she washed his truck and stocked his trailer with food and a fly swatter.

- Leroy was strange. Amanda decided it would be safer to date a guy with bullet holes in his mailbox.

- Max taught me a welcoming Spanish phrase before my trip to Mexico. Turns out it translated to "Don't f--- with me, buddy." I used it on a taxi driver who dropped me off, with luggage, at a food cart instead of my hotel.

- My pills are a different size and shape with each refill. I worry they're hormones and I'll grow a mustache.

EXAMPLE OF HUMOR IN MEMOIR

In Praise of Men in Uniform

Thing 1 and Thing 2 were coming for a visit, which required preparations: meds relocated, furniture turned into blockades, corner cushions applied to glass table tops, and an alarm set on balcony doors. This was so a *ding, ding, ding* signaled when orders not to pet Coco (a squirrel) were ignored. And carseats had to be installed.

This last task seemed simple enough, but I watched my son-in-law perform this function one day and concluded that, for me, it would be a physical, mental, and mechanical challenge equivalent to overhauling a motor. But as Grandma GoGo, a woman determined to ensure the safety of precious, pug-nosed, pudgy-legged little criminals, I got on my I-am-woman-watch-me-roar mentality and prepared for the task. This meant eating all the bacon I wanted and mustering the courage and determination to, by god, install carseats.

I dug them out of the tornado shelter, which was stuffed so full that, if I had to get in there, something would have to come out. Intimidating belts and hooks dangled from the seats, suggesting menacing mechanical requirements—not my forte. Perplexing instruction manuals did nothing to mitigate my interpretation of the situation. In spite of the gloomy prospects, I made a good go of it. No sentence enhancers were used in the process, in spite of a level of frustration equal to the experience of parallel parking. These efforts failed, and reality prevailed. No amount of bacon could equip GoGo for the challenge of installing carseats. So off I went to Fire Station 4.

Under the impression, from a news report, that firemen would check out carseat installations as a civic duty, I pulled up in front of Station 4. Men in uniforms—navy T-shirts adorned with gold emblems and matching pants— crawled like ants all over a red firetruck, polishing and pampering. Bruce Springsteen blasted from some source, and the energy of the young, fit men was palpable. As I approached, several of them looked at me curiously. They must have wondered what this old lady was up to. A young hunk asked, "Can we help you?"

I put on my best and well-practiced begging and pleading routine. "I'm old, please help me. My grandchildren are arriving at the airport today, and I have a dilemma. I'm picking them up, and I can't get these frigging carseats installed. I've been told you fellows check out carseat installations. Clearly, I have failed. Can you help me?"

"I'm sorry, ma'am. We only do that on certain days and at another station."

I looked pathetic. Desperate. Downtrodden. "Oh, my, what shall I do? They're arriving in a few hours."

An attractive young man dropped from the top of the firetruck and approached. "I've got kids. I'm a carseat aficionado. Let's take a look."

In a matter of seconds, four gorgeous, uniformed man-butts protruded from all four doors of my vehicle as carseats were wrestled into proper positions and secured so tightly they would not budge a millimeter under any circumstance. I smiled.

"That should do it, ma'am."

"Indeed."

I wanted to hug all of them, or perhaps ravage them, but I exercised extreme self-discipline, thanked them profusely, and went on my way. As I pulled out of the driveway, the vision of Tulsa's finest mounting that firetruck to resume their duties was reflected in the rear-view mirror. I concluded I had just been blessed with a near-sex experience extraordinaire.

After Thing 1 and Thing 2 left, a week later, I realized the carseats were so solidly installed there was no way I could uninstall them.

Oh darn. Off I went to Fire Station 4.

* * *

Later, when thinking back on the situation, I became so impassioned over the adorable young men intent on rescue that I wrote a poem in their honor:

A Man in Uniform

Oh, hi.

If you write a page a day, you'll write a book in a year.—Bonnie Hearn Hill, *The Writer* magazine, August 2019

Chapter 17

WRITING—THE FOREVER GIFT

Writing is a canvas for gifting and self-actualization.

The simple gesture of sharing a composition fosters seeds of hope and joy for generations. It can change lives. But first, you have to write it. As a writer, you make a difference when you create something, whether it is fiction or nonfiction; whether it is through books, short stories, essays, poetry, or whatever. Compositions that enhance the lives of others take you to the pinnacle of achievement.

MEMOIR AS A GIFT: Earlier, I talked about redefining success. Consider yourself successful when you turn your writing into a gift. Let me make a case for sharing your life experiences and wisdom through memoir. In this scenario, success is guaranteed because memoir creates legacy, and legacies are forever.

Gandhi said, "Your life is your message." Many people write their life stories and put them in a drawer. Lives can be hugely influenced for generations by a chronicled personal history. Sharing yours while you are still here allows descendants to ask questions and to revel in your experiences, which is a blessing to you and them. Such stories build strong generational connections and give a precious and enduring gift to those you care about most and to others you don't even know or who are not born yet.

> When you capture a life story (yours or someone else's), relatives develop a sense of their heritage. Descendants will do the same years from now. They may never experience the time and place where their ancestors lived, but they will know that time and place. They may never meet the persons whose stories you tell, but they will know them. Documented stories live forever. (*Capture Life—Write a Memoir,* Nikki Hanna)

Frame your definition of success around that scenario, and your writing experience will be purposeful. Among all the incredible things you write, consider memoir one of them.

BEING GENEROUS AND BRAVE: Your writing gift may be less personal than memoir, but it can be just as powerful. Whether you write to entertain, inform, encourage the troubled, celebrate the fortunate, or tickle the fancy of fans of fiction or fantasy, what you write is yours and yours alone. No one else can create that gift or give it. Only you can express what is within you. Be generous and courageous. Share your lessons learned and your wondrous, exceptional, imperfect self through what you write.

Writing is hard. In addition to creative challenges, writers must deal with issues of English and grammar.

> This includes such things as verb infinitives; helping verbs; irregular verbs; transitive and

intransitive verbs; gerunds; collective nouns; coordinating conjunctions; demonstrative and interrogative pronouns; direct and indirect objects; positive, comparative, and superlative adjectives; singular and plural antecedents; restrictive and nonrestrictive clauses; and simple and complex nouns and predicates, to name a few.

It would be easier to learn Swahili or Zulu than to learn the nuances of the English language. In her book, *100 Writing Mistakes to Avoid*, Maeve Maddox gives comfort in this regard. She says, "You don't have to know how to build an internal combustion engine to drive a car, but you do have to know such terms as *steering wheel, brake pedal*, and *hood release*." Grammar is like that.

So, if someone insinuates that, as a writer, you should be able to determine whether to use lie, lying, or lain because you understand the concepts of imperative, present declarative, present continuous, and past participle, know that you don't. You just need a good editor. Don't be intimidated by grammar.

WHAT MATTERS: Many frustrations writers face are primarily derived from failing to consciously decide what is important. Noise in the writing environment is intense. It tells writers what they must or should do or what they should care about.

What matters is best determined by the writer himself based on desired goals and outcomes. For example, writing craft doesn't matter so much if you are writing simply for the enjoyment of the process. Craft might matter some if you plan to share your writing, depending on whether you care about impressing readers. Craft matters for sure if you plan to publish what you write.

Know why you write so you know what matters. Then, shut out the rest of the hubbub and find your own path.

LISTEN UP, WRITER: When your confidence is threatened; when you experience crushing disappointments (and you will); when you conclude that what you wrote is a conglomeration of useless, disjointed works; and when you are on the cusp of giving up on writing, don't lose your emotional compass. Out of that chaos is a work of art waiting to be freed from disorder—one you, and only you, can resurrect. Once you pull it out, wrestle it down, and shape it into all it can be, fling it into the universe and know that you matter.

June Carter Cash was asked by a friend, "What are you up to these days?" She responded, "I'm just trying to matter." Writing is a way to matter. When you write, you accomplish much more than just engaging readers.

- Peers look at you with respect, and they are inspired.

- Friends and relatives look at you in awe.

- Other writers look at you and are encouraged.

- Younger people observe you and view their futures and the process of aging more positively.

- Children and grandchildren discover you are way cooler than they thought. (What is more important than that?)

Through writing, you create legacy and hope. What's more, you become a positive role model. That might be the most important thing you do on your writing and aging journey.

Bethany, my three-year-old granddaughter, found one of my books and noticed my picture on the back cover.

Her mother explained that GoGo had written it. Bethany carried the book around all day, studied the pictures, and pretended to read it. The book ended up in the toy box, standing ready for another pretend time.

That book may mean more to Bethany than to anyone else who has a copy. Perhaps it will spark in her a lifelong fascination with books, or maybe she will write her own book someday because her grandma did. When I contemplate her playtime adventure with my book, I know I am a successful author. And I know I matter.

My wish for you, dear writer, is that through what you create, you matter. I hope you find purpose in writing, develop a deep understanding of why you write, define success on your own terms, and discover a niche compatible with your innate talents. I hope you customize the principles of craft to your situation, appreciate their value, realize the power and magic of your words, and relish the legacy you create by sharing them.

I hope that, through uninhibited self-expression and the path you take to share your creations, you shine and sparkle. I hope you produce something incredible that causes you to take your hands off the keyboard, lean back in your ergonomically correct chair topped with a pillow, thrust clenched fists in the air, and shout, "Y-E-E-S-S!"

If you are discouraged with the outcome of a piece, I hope you start the next one. I hope that through your creations you foster seeds of hope and joy for generations. I hope you develop a sense of purposefulness, and that you know, unequivocally, that you matter. I wish for you all of that. So write you promising, spirited, driven, crazy-wonderful writer. Write, and be joyful.

****

Vocabulary and grammar are your primary tools. They're most effectively used, even most effectively abused, by people who understand them.—Octavio E. Butler, Bloodchild and Other Stories

APPENDIX

RUN-THROUGH LAYERING PROCESS

This technique involves going over a working draft numerous times during the revision phase of writing. (Do this *after* the draft's structure is organized, the writing is substantially developed, and *before* editing.)

This process is called *layering*. Each run-through focuses on one or several compatible objectives (listed below). Every pass adds another level of depth and shine. The piece becomes increasingly robust. Some run-throughs go quickly. Others require considerable time. Some are not necessary for certain projects or for seasoned writers.

If the layering process is intimidating, keep this in mind: Going over and over a manuscript and refining it is revision, and *revision is writing.* (If any of the following terms or rules are unfamiliar, google them.)

- **Establish a premise and an overall theme.** Introduce the theme and premise (message), or at least hint at them, in the first chapter. Thread the theme throughout (don't overdo). Zap it at the end. Subthemes can be incorporated throughout or limited to certain chapters. Tie them to the main theme, if they are compatible. Resolve the major theme and confirm the composition's message at the end.

- **Create structure.** For fiction, consider outlining the story or building a storyboard to create a narrative arc. Although the arc is a fiction-writing concept, memoir is often story-like and can benefit from such an arc. For nonfiction, an outline and/or a table of contents help arrange content into a logical sequence. Do this after the first draft is completed and the content is reasonably determined. Structure is fluid. Revise the arc or table of contents as needed.

- **Organize.** Create a beginning, middle, and end for the book and for each chapter and scene.

- **Establish flow and manage pace.** Build up low spots. Don't let the middle slump—up the stakes, increase the action, or introduce subplots. Surprise the reader—even shock him. Keep in mind, though, that continuous emotion or action exhausts the reader. Spread out action. To slow things down, insert exposition, narration, or dialogue. As in music, mellow points make the dynamic ones more effective. Apply intensity in waves.

- **Determine verb tense:** Ensure consistency of tense. Intentional variations are appropriate—if they don't jolt or confuse readers. Tense changes create layers of time. Note: If you use *had* or *would* often (a common practice of novice writers), reconsider the tense in which you write. Tense is complicated. Research it online.

- **Manage point of view (POV).** Establish POV in the first few sentences of the book and in the beginning of each chapter and scene. Avoid head-hopping (shifting POV from one person to another within a scene or chapter) unless doing so strategically. Clue the reader in on changes.

- **Add dialogue.** Use conversation to describe characters, to move the story forward, and to break up exposition and narrative. Dialogue and the actions surrounding it are *show, don't tell* opportunities. Sprinkle them throughout. Make certain all dialogue is concise and relevant.

- **Create tension/conflict.** Include these in every chapter through characters' internal and external conflicts. Have characters want something they cannot get.

- **Use names effectively.** Avoid overusing first and last name combinations after initially introducing a character's full name. Pick the first or last one and use it. In fiction, use the point-of-view character's full name the first time you mention him or her. Then use third person (he or she) for that person for most of the rest of a scene or chapter.

- **Use names to define characters.** Names do a lot of work. Select names that supply information about characters—their cultures, ages, temperaments, etc. Imply details through names. Keep a list of unique, interesting ones. Even minor characters need revealing names—a mechanic named Ode, a woman named Roxie, a dog named Rufus. Ensure that names reflect the genre and category of a piece.

- **Develop characters and construct character arcs.** Primary characters should evolve—change over time. Make them complex, flawed, and sympathetic—even the bad guys. Describe internal and external characteristics. Give people special abilities, unusual traits, temperaments, grievances, hopes, vulnerabilities, strengths, weaknesses, relationships, regrets, and losses. Give them histories and physical attributes. Note how they move. Define their essences (ways of being in the world). Make every character, no matter how minor, interesting—no cardboard characters.

- **Show, don't tell.** Replace commentary with dialogue, behavior, expressions, or actions where possible. In general, avoid using "tell" words, such as *feel, felt, knew, seemed, noticed, looked, saw, heard, learned, realized, wondered, guessed, hoped,* or *thought.* But know that, for expediency, sometimes it is best to tell through narration or exposition. Telling is not wrong.

- **Add quotes.** In nonfiction, quotes give authority to premise and content. They also add flavor and interest.

- **Use thought shots.** Thoughts of characters, presented in italics, reveal information and introduce a stylistic quality.

- **Use spotlights.** These are short, pithy, dramatic statements that add interest. (Examples: *It freed his freak. Mom went gangster.*) Avoid overdoing. Keep them special.

- **Describe vivid settings.** Readers need a sense of time, place, and environment in every scene. Settings add context. Paint pictures with words. Describe environments, cultures, noises, terrains, structures, and possessions. Establish geography, climate, history, social context, and the time and season of events. Don't overdo, though, and don't present setting information all at once in a data dump.

- **Make minor events, major.** Take tidbits to a higher level. Share a wider, more global (universal) perspective where possible. (For example: "Every woman in the room knew it could happen to her.") Make the inconsequential, consequential. Embellish with absorbing details and meaning. This is an opportunity to stand out as a writer.

- **Interject humor.** Apply comedic techniques. For example, carry a joke full circle and use it again in the ending (referred to as a callback). Repeat a character's humorous habit. Develop colorful, quirky characters. Don't be afraid of self-deprecating humor. Make your readers laugh.

- **Evaluate passive voice.** Consider changing passive voice sentences into active ones. Passive voice is not wrong, but writing is generally stronger and more efficient with active voice.

- **Tap into the senses:** Include at least one sensory description in every scene. Go beyond the visual. Don't forget the often overlooked taste, smell, touch, and the sixth sense, intuition.

- **Introduce sentiment.** Weave in emotions. Express spiritual connections, passions, and relationships with people, animals, and nature. Deepen relationships. Give characters pets.

- **Manage the "person" factor.** Be cognizant of singular and plural uses (*he/she* or *they/them*). The too-frequent use of *I, me, my, myself* in memoir and other first-person writing is distracting and can insinuate self-indulgence. They are important words, but rewrite to eliminate them where possible. When writing in second person for nonfiction how-to or instructional books, take out *you* and *your* where possible. But remember, these words are necessary. They are not wrong. They bring the writer closer to the reader.

- **Enhance voice.** Express a unique author's voice. Build descriptions of events and scenes in clever, unusual ways. Express yourself freely without intruding on the story. Make every sentence, paragraph, and page better and more enticing. Don't leave a page until it is robust with voice.

- **Assess metaphors, similes, and clichés.** Use original ones. Don't overdo. Too many inhibit their effect and shout "amateur." In general, avoid clichés. They tend to be trite. In most cases, your own fabulous, fresh words are best.

- **Enhance specificity of detail.** Paint a picture with words. Don't overdo. Make readers feel. Say *aspen tree* instead of *tree*. Say *shadowy* figures, *pulsating* music, *soft* wind, *polite* rain, *grinding* hurt, or a *weeping, ordained* warrior woman. Find a balance between expressive writing and adjective use.

- **Use adjectives cautiously.** Pay attention to the overuse of adjectives. Stacking adjectives can be a stylistic feature, but it can also suggest amateur writing, especially if more than two are used. Stacking sometimes happens when the writer is over-writing or he didn't find the right noun. Stronger nouns often make adjectives unnecessary.

- **Punctuate adjectives correctly.** When using two or more adjectives, a comma between them may be required. If you can insert an *and* between the adjectives or reverse their order, separate them with a comma. For example, *an outstanding, famous speaker.*

- **Eliminate adverbs.** Occasionally, I'll run across an expert who defends the use of adverbs, but this is rare. Verbs are usually stronger without them. Sometimes you've got to use an adverb, but experts suggest that they be avoided when possible. Usually three or four to a book is appropriate. If a word ends in *–ly*, consider taking it out.

- **Tighten up.** Assess the value of every word. Don't use unnecessary or redundant ones. Avoid stating the obvious. Remove redundant sentences and paragraphs.

- **Avoid empty words.** Avoid *some, any, the, that, even, just,* and *all* where possible. In the case of *it, they, them, this, item, thing,* and *something,* consider substituting more descriptive words. These words are not wrong and are okay to use, but do so judiciously. It is best to avoid starting a sentence with *There is* or *There are* when possible.

- **Evaluate word selection.** These words are distractions: *very, really, literally, pretty,* and *basically.* Eliminate them. Don't use a big word when a simple one will do.

221

Ensure words match dictionary definitions. If you can't think of a perfect word, use a thesaurus. Don't use an important word twice (called an "echo") in a sentence or paragraph. Don't use unique, flashy words or phrases (*pizzazz, extraordinaire, trepidation*) more than two or three times in a book unless they're theme related.

- **Emphasize words or phrases.** Use *quotation marks, italics*, and *boldface* for emphasis in nonfiction. Rarely are these appropriate in fiction or in story-like memoir. They distract from the story. Avoid underlining.

- **Improve paragraphs.** Analyze each paragraph. Consider using this popular method of organization: Place the most important sentence at the beginning of a paragraph. Make it topical—on point. Then, have every sentence after that support or embellish it. Avoid redundant sentences (sentences that say the same thing in different ways). Assess the order of sentences. Make the last one a clarifying statement, a summarizing point, or a potent snippet. Use it to transition smoothly to the next paragraph.

- **Improve sentences.** Go over every sentence and endeavor to improve it. Consider its structure and its proper place in a paragraph or manuscript. Vary sentence structure. Starting every sentence with a noun is boring. The poetry concept of putting important or strong words at the end of lines applies to sentences as well. Make sentences more tight, rhythmic, or remarkable.

- **Elliptical sentences:** Writers can intentionally leave out words with the expectation readers will fill them in. For example, Ray was a cautious driver; Mandy, a maniac on the road. Use a semicolon after the first sentence and a comma in place of the missing verb.

- **Enhance the format.** Introduce white space. Break up long paragraphs. Vary paragraph size. In nonfiction, create white space through formatting. Use bullets. Insert lists. A space between paragraphs is appropriate for nonfiction. Some experts recommend that all chapters be similar in size.

- **Create transitions.** Ensure flow sentence to sentence, paragraph to paragraph, and chapter to chapter. Leave chapters with teasers—an intriguing thought, a profound question, a high or low point—or a precarious one. Delaying resolution until the next chapter encourages readers to read on, but every chapter doesn't have to end in a cliffhanger.

- **Avoid split infinitives.** Although commonly used today, split infinitives are grammatically incorrect. Few readers pick up on them, but grammarians do. Google the concept. The *to* should be next to the verb. Example: It is incorrect to say *How to Not Write Like an Amateur.* Instead, say, *How Not to Write Like an Amateur.*

- **Check spelling.** Read the manuscript aloud, word by word or even syllable by syllable. Verify spelling of questionable words. Don't rely on a spell checker, grammar software, or autocorrect. (If it changes *sentence* to *suntan,* or *composite characters* to *compost characters*, or *ergonomically* to *economically*, you'll be shocked; and your readers, confused. Trust me, I know.)

- **Meet Genre/Category Requirements.** Genre categories are broad. Each has tried and true approaches. Children's books, in particular, have specific requirements. Learn the best practices of the category in which you write.

FIND-AND-FIX SWEEPS PROCESS

The following craft recommendations don't always mean alternatives are wrong, and some rules are controversial among experts. Also, there are reasons to break rules. Writers often violate them in the interest of style, practicality, and creativity. In general, though, complying with rules of craft is a gift to readers, and compliance is important to agents, publishers, and contest judges. Avoid controversial craft issues in the first few pages of a document where you want to demonstrate your mastery of craft.

Use a computer Find capability to sweep the document for opportunities to improve craft. Below are the most common *find-and-fix* opportunities. It would be a major task to search all of them, and one would have to question your sanity if you did so. However, reviewing this list will help you recognize what to watch out for. Focus on those important to you and on those you tend to use improperly. (If any of the following terms or rules are unfamiliar, google them for details.)

REVIEW FOR POSSIBLE DELETION OR SUBSTITUTION

Put the following words on trial. They are not wrong. Most are common words used in every book or composition, including this one. But they are often trite, overused, unnecessary, or they cry out for better words. Some are out of favor with writing experts, agents, and publishers. Search for them, assess them, and take them out or rewrite to avoid them where you deem appropriate.

Words to reconsider: *that, the, now, then, still, yet, well, just, get, got, even, must, any, all, some, rather, quite, kind of, sort of, most, almost, a little, a lot, somewhat, just about, really, pretty, very.* For example, "It is *hard*" is stronger than "It is *really hard, pretty hard,* or *very hard."* Or there is a better word as in the following examples:

- instead of v*ery noisy,* use *deafening*
- instead of v*ery open,* use *transparent*
- instead of v*ery often,* use *frequently*
- instead of v*ery painful,* use *excruciating.*

Adverbs: Use sparingly. Search for words ending in *–ly* and reconsider them. Examples: *practically, virtually, roughly, relatively, moderately, slightly, fairly, clearly, nearly, truly, actually, certainly, literally, suddenly.* Verbs and sentences are generally stronger without these words. (An adverb can be placed either before or after a verb.)

Might, may, maybe, perhaps, probably: When you've got to use them, do so judiciously.

The fact is, as a matter of fact, or **in order to:** In general, it's best to avoid using these. They are filler phrases.

Never, always, or **every:** Use only when the word is literally true.

Had, has, would, should, could: These can suggest verb tense or strength issues. Write "Dad stoked the fire," not "Dad *would* stoke the fire." If using *had* or *would* often, examine the tense in which you write. (Google *past perfect tense.*)

It, there, this, they, thing, something, item: These are *empty* or *dummy* words. Consider more descriptive ones.

Basically, totally, and the vernacular **like:** Avoid using these words, even in conversation—unless you're quoting someone on spring break at Panama Beach, Florida.

Like (in simile): When part of a simile, *like* is a good word to use, but don't overdo it. Alternatives are: *as, as though, as if,* and *similar to.* (Using too many similes or metaphors weakens their impact and is amateurish.)

Echoes: Don't repeat common words that are in close proximity to each other. Don't repeat important words within a paragraph. Don't use flashy, uncommon words more than once in a chapter or more than two or three times in a book unless they are theme related.

Tried to, started to, began to: Unless the person only just tried, started, or began, but didn't go beyond that, get down to what happened. For example, say "She cried" instead of "She began to cry."

Feel, felt, seemed, noticed, looked, saw, heard, knew, learned, thought, realized, wondered, guessed, hoped: You might be *telling* when s*howing* is better. Show through action, behavior, expression, or dialogue. And don't use emojis to *show* unless you're or a preadolescent.

Prepositional phrases: These are okay—even good—to use, but keep them to a minimum, especially in compound sentences. Sweep for the most common prepositions (*of, to, in, by,* and *for*) and reevaluate.

–ing words: Some writers overuse words ending in *–ing.* Beginning a sentence with an *–ing* word is okay occasionally to vary sentence structure, but don't do it too often.

REVIEW FOR GOOD CRAFT

Person: Check for consistency of person. Some shifts in person are appropriate, but execute them so readers aren't jolted.

First person: *I, my, me, we, us, our, ours*
Second person: *you, your, yours*
Third person: *he, him, his, she, her, hers, they, them, their*

Active or passive voice: Sweep for the passive verbs *be, being, been, was, were, are,* and *is*. These are not bad words, and you cannot write without them. They do suggest possible passive voice, though. Consider using active voice. Passive voice is not wrong, but active voice is stronger and more efficient. (**Passive:** The house was painted by Ed. **Active:** Ed painted the house.)

Quotation marks: Sweep to ensure periods and commas are *always* inside closing quotation marks. Question marks and exclamation marks are inside or outside of quotation marks, depending on whether or not they are part of the quote.

Question marks: Search for *who, what, why, when, where, how,* and *do,* and check for question marks. A rhetorical question (one that does not require an answer or one asked just to make a point) does not need a question mark. In these cases, the author's intent determines whether a question mark is used. Never use multiple questions marks (???).

Spacing after periods: Search for two spaces at the end of sentences. Reduce them to one.

Indention: Whether or not to indent the first paragraph after a chapter title or a major heading is a choice. Style-guide requirements vary. Adhere to your publisher's preferences.

GRAMMAR RULES
AND WRITING PRINCIPLES

Grammar rules represent a shared understanding through the general agreement of most experts. Writing principles define what agents, publishers, judges, seasoned writers, and most readers look for when assessing a writer's work. Apply rules and principles when doing revision, editing, run-throughs, and sweeps. The following rules and principles are ones with which novice writers struggle. Some are too complex to cover in detail here. Explore them in more depth through an Internet search. (Google can be a writer's best friend.) And make sure you have a good editor.

This, That/These, Those/Which, Who:

This or *that/these* or *those* - Usage is determined by proximity in time or space. *This* and *these* are close and suggests present tense. *That* and *those* are distant or in the past.

That or *which* - *That* is used when the clause is required for the sentence to make sense (restrictive clause—it must be there). *That* **is not** preceded by a comma. *Which* is used when the sentence makes sense without the clause information. (It is nonrestrictive—not necessary.) *Which* **is** preceded by a comma.

That or *who* - Use *who* (not *that*) when referring to people. Use *that* when referring to a company, event, or a thing. Controversy exists when it comes to animals. The trend is to use *who* if the animal has a close relationship and a name. Otherwise, use *it* or *that*. (A skunk is most likely an *it*. A pet a *who*.)

It's or **Its:** *It's* is a contraction for *it is*, while *its* shows possession. (Consider replacing *it* with a more descriptive word.)

Who or **Whom:** Some consider *whom* too formal. It rarely sounds right since most people don't use it in speech. (If you use *whom*, mentally reword the sentence to determine if it's appropriate. If *him* or *her* sounds right, use *whom*. If *he* or *she* sounds right, use *who*.) Use *whom* when it's the object of a verb or preposition unless it sounds awkward, which it sometimes does.

Lay(s), Laid, Laying: To *lay* means to put down an object, person, or an animal. (Lay down the baby.)

Lie(s), Lay(s), Lain, Lying: To *lie* means to recline or rest. (Lie here for a while.)

If or **Whether:** Use *if* for conditions and w*hether* for choices.

However or **Nevertheless:** Both show contrast between two sentences or clauses. *Nevertheless* is more formal.

Can, May, or **Might:** *Can* relates to ability; *may* to permission. Technically, *may* is present tense and *might* is past; however, it's generally accepted to use them interchangeably.

Shall or **Will:** Technically, use *shall* with first person (I/we); and *will* with all others. (Shall is rarely used in American English.)

Awhile or **A While:** *Awhile* is an adverb that means *for a time*. *A while* is a noun phrase that means *over a period of time*. (Insert "for" in front of *awhile*. If it works, use *a while*.)

Of: Don't say *off of;* just say *off.* (Unless it just doesn't sound right.) *Could of* should be *could have. Out of* is okay to use.

Into or **In To:** *Into* is a preposition expressing motion. *In to* is part of a verb phrase.

Onto is a preposition. **On to** is a phrase meaning move on.

i.e. or **e.g.:** *i.e.* means *in other words*; *e.g.* means *for example.* Experts disagree over the usage and punctuation of these. Alternative: use *that is* for i.e. and *for example* for *e.g.*

I, **Me**, **My**, **Myself:** These are placed last when used with another person. (*Mike and I* or *My friends and me.*) Rules for *my* and *myself* are tricky. Google them.

You're or **Your:** *You're* is the contraction for *you are.* *Your* shows possession. (Seems everyone should know this, but how many times have you seen these used incorrectly on social media?)

They're, Their, or **There:** *They're* is the contraction for *they are. Their* reflects *possession/ownership. There* refers to *a place.* (Seems everyone should know this, but how many times, have you seen. . . .) Consider replacing these with more descriptive words.

There is or **There are:** The verb *is* or *are* is determined by whether the object of that verb is singular or plural. (Singular object: *There is one cabin.* Plural object: *There are many cabins.*) Rewrite to avoid starting a sentence with these words when possible. It's best not to use them on the first pages, where you want to show mastery of craft.

Fewer or **Less:** *Fewer* refers to a number (can be counted). *Less* means a measurement (time, distance, amount).

Good or Well: *Good* is an adjective; *well,* an adverb.

Forty and **Ninety:** These words are commonly misspelled as *fourty* and *ninty.*

Alright or **All Right:** *Alright* is not a generally accepted word—yet. (It is trending.) Use a*ll right.*

All Ready or **Already:** *All ready* means *fully prepared.* *Already* means *previously.*

Non-words: Don't use a*nyways, everywheres, nowheres, hisself, irregardless, inbetween, theirselves, alright, ain't, alot* unless in dialogue where such words reflect a character's lack of refinement.

Affect or **Effect:** *Affect* is a verb. *Effect* is usually a noun.

Round, Around, or **A Round:** *Round* refers to *a shape,* or it can be a verb that creates *a not exact number. Around* refers to *in the area of.* In general, avoid using *a round* unless referring to *a round of poker or some such activity.*

Backward(s) and **Afterward(s):** The plural versions, are British English. The singular versions are fairly standard in American English. Neither are wrong. Be consistent.

However, Therefore, Nevertheless, Furthermore, Moreover: When used to join compound sentences, use a semicolon before and a comma after. In other cases when used in a sentence, a comma before and after is appropriate. When used at the start of a sentence, put a comma after.

Similar sounding words with different meanings: Such words are often used incorrectly. A large number of them exist. Here are a few: *who's/whose, chose/choose, loose/ lose, bear/bare, breath/breathe, allusion/illusion, accept/ except, lead/led, aide/aid.* When questioning which word to use, google words this way: f*urther* vs *farther.*

Parallel phrasing: Make the phrasing of each item in a series structurally compatible by starting each one the same way, for example, "I'm going to style my hair, paint my nails, and dress to the nines." (Each phrase starts with a verb.) Also, use compatible structure in compound sentences where possible. Proper parallel writing is one sign of an expert. Google *parallel phrasing.*

A series: If possible, put the shortest phrase in a series first and the longest one last (perhaps making it a zinger). Use the Oxford comma (the comma in a series before the *and* or *or*).

Quote or quotation: Technically, *quote* is a verb and *quotation* a noun. However, in modern writing, they are used interchangeably, with *quote* being the most common.

Possessive: If a plural word or name ends in an *s*, some experts suggest using only an apostrophe to make it possessive and dropping the second *s* (*Chris' car* rather than *Chris's car*). If two or more people possess something, show possession with the last one. (*Ann and Dale's car.*)

I-before-E rule: These words don't follow the rule "*i* before *e,* except after *c* or when sounding like *a*": *weird, being, foreign, caffeine, either, feisty, height, leisure, protein, science, ancient, reimburse, seize, sovereign, species, society,* and *sufficient.*

Redundant words: A word that repeats the meaning of another word is redundant and should be eliminated, such as *free gift, add up, general public, gather together, frozen ice, added bonus, absolutely certain, foreign imports, first and foremost, exact same, current trend, completely surrounded, collaborate together, close proximity, circulate around, ATM machine,* and *brief moment.*

Dangling or **misplaced participles:** Verbs ending in *–ing* or *–ed* that serve as adjectives by modifying nouns or pronouns are called participles. When a participle or a participial phrase acts as an adjective to modify a noun or a noun phrase, use it with care, or you could end up with something like this: *Abraham Lincoln wrote the Gettysburg*

Address while traveling from Washington to Gettysburg on the back of an envelope. This is a complicated grammatical issue. Google it. Or make sure you have a good editor.

Subject-verb agreement: If the subject is plural, the verb has no *s*. If the subject is singular, the verb has an *s,* for example, *They run. He runs. Were* is used with a plural subject (They were); and *was,* with a singular subject (He was). Exception: When a *condition* is involved, use were (*If* he *were*).

Gender-neutral writing: It is generally accepted now to use the plural pronouns, *them, their,* and *they* to avoid gender-specific singular pronouns (*he, him, she,* and *her*). However, experts disagree on this point.

Tense and **person:** Most fiction today is written in limited (one person's perspective) third person (he, she) past tense (was, were). Readers are so accustomed to this that they don't notice it. Memoir is usually written in first person (I, me) past tense (*was* or verbs ending in *–ed*). Studying tense and person will make your head hurt, I promise, but these concepts are critical to good craft and are often done wrong. Google for details.

Split infinitives: The rule not to split infinitives is not strictly followed today. A notorious example of a split infinitive is *Star Trek's* "to boldly go." Technically, it should be "to go boldly" so the adverb is not between *to* and *go.* Most readers will not pick up on split infinitives, but grammarians will. It's best to avoid them (split infinitives, not grammarians) in formal writing, on book covers, or in the first few pages of any document where it is important to demonstrate mastery of craft.

Dialogue tags: Avoid descriptive tags and use *he said/she said* (or *asked/responded*) most of the time. Put the tag *after* the dialogue unless it is long. (Avoid long dialogue.) Some experts recommend putting the name or personal pronoun first (Ed *said* rather than *said Ed)*. In a two-way conversation, don't use tags after the first time each person speaks. If more than two people are talking, occasional tags may be required to clarify who's speaking. Develop characters so readers know who's talking by how they speak.

Capitalization: Titles, such as *Mom, Dad, Aunt,* and *Uncle* are capitalized, except when preceded by *a, an, my,* or *our*. For example, "We visited Dad." or "We visited my dad."

Exclamation marks: Don't use these merely to make a point or for emphasis. Use for surprise, excitement, shouting, or strong emotions. Amateurs commonly overuse them. Never use more than one in a row (!!!).

Periods: William Zinsser said, "There's not much to say about the period except that most writers don't reach it soon enough." Use one space after a period.

Commas: If you want to enjoy a grammar argument online, look up whether to use a comma before *that, because, as, since,* or *as well*. I don't use one. Whatever you decide to do, apply the rule consistently. Use a comma before *such as* but none after when it is followed by an example. Use a comma after introductory prepositional phrases (optional if less than four words). Don't use a comma when writing only the month and year (June 2016).

Punctuating compound sentences: *But, and, so, yet,* and *or* are coordinating conjunctions usually connecting two complete sentences into a compound sentence. If both sentences have a subject and a verb, the conjunction is preceded by a comma. If not, don't use a comma.

- *Harry hid the gun, but he didn't hide it well enough.*

- *Harry hid the gun but didn't hide it well enough.*

It's generally acceptable to start a sentence with a conjunction, but don't overdo, and don't do so on the first few pages of a piece where you want to demonstrate craft.

Punctuating compound-complex sentences: This is when two complete sentences are combined and at least one of them contains another clause that cannot stand alone as a sentence. Three ways to punctuate are acceptable. Be consistent.

- *Harry hid the gun, but, on this occasion, he didn't hide it well enough.* (formal—I learned this in 1962, but with a semicolon after *gun*)

- *Harry hid the gun, but on this occasion, he didn't hide it well enough.* (trendy)

- *Harry hid the gun but, on this occasion, he didn't hide it well enough.* (trending)

Save yourself and break compound-complex sentences into two separate ones so punctuation is not an issue.

Hyphens, *en* dashes, and *em* dashes: A hyphen is the shorter of these three (-) and is used to combine words and set apart numbers.

An *en* dash represents the size of a typesetter's letter *n* (–) and means "through" or that letters are left out as in *–ing*.

The em dash represents the size of the letter *m* (—). It's used to show an interruption, to replace commas (for emphasis), or to suggest "more to come." It is also used between a quote and the author's name. Substituting *two hyphens* for an *em* dash is not wrong, but it's more professional to use the *em* dash. Most computers have a function for generating *en* and *em* dashes." (Google *dashes.*)

Do not put a space before or after a hyphen or dash.

Ellipses (. . .): This indicates an omission, pause, or trailing off. Spacing is a matter of preference. Be consistent. A fourth point acts as a period. *He is smart—above average. . . .*

A STORY AUTOPSY

A short story I wrote, "Rich Man's Sport," incorporates many of the writing principles and practices covered in this book. The "autopsy" following it identifies and illustrates them.

A run-through was done during revision of this story focused entirely on eliminating unnecessary words. That process made the writing tighter and more efficient.

The underlined words in this story signal that they were not in earlier drafts. Rather, they were added during multiple revision run-throughs. These enhancements demonstrate how important revision is to polishing a story, particularly to adding voice.

Rich Man's Sport

(1)...Dust billows behind <u>brawny</u> trucks <u>decorated with logos</u> and pulling <u>showy</u>, oversized trailers loaded with horses and howling dogs. Chance sits on the front steps of the bunkhouse, <u>rubbing the stubble from his first shave</u> and observing the procession rumbling down the Oklahoma ranch road. Wealthy men drive the trucks. Fussy, blond women in <u>fancy</u> boots and jeans <u>decorated with sparkles</u> ride shotgun. Chance doesn't care for such women. They remind him of those he meets when he visits his mother in Tulsa—women with long, polished fingernails who drink wine <u>and wear jewelry to swimming pools</u>.

(2) Blue chases the trailers. No amount of scolding stops her. She is mostly an outdoor dog, and Dad rarely lets her in the bunkhouse. So Chance gives up on discipline and allows her to run back and forth between the bunkhouse and the ranch clubhouse where a hunt is being staged.

236

Because of the trucks, horses, and dogs, she goes nuts on hunt days.

(3) Blue was a puppy when the ranch's owner gave her to Chance after his mom left. Purebred blue heelers are valuable, so Chance understood right off that she was special. Sometimes he sleeps with her outside in the bed of Dad's old Ford truck or in a sleeping bag in the yard. It is there that Chance worships stars, like real cowboys did years ago on cattle drives, and hopes ticks have a preference for herding dogs.

(4) Chance disapproves of the rich man's hunt. Participants invade the ranch on weekends and gallop through pastures on purebred horses, pursuing bellowing hounds on the trail of newly released coyotes. These wealthy men rate this sport on the level of a fox hunt. Chance considers it a joke. He likes the hounds, though, and loves romping with them.

(5) His dad slams the screen door, whacks Chance playfully on the back of the head, and strides cowboy-like toward the ranch clubhouse, swinging a sack of mountain oysters. The ranch hands will fry them up for lunch and attempt to convince naive guests the testicles are chicken nuggets.

(6) Later, as Chance munches on breakfast cereal, he spots Blue out of the kitchen window, nipping at the heels of a bull in the pasture. Roscoe is disinterested. He's king of the world, and he knows it. *Good luck, Blue.*

Although less than a year old, Blue has proven to be a good herder. She herded a bunch of partiers on the patio at the main ranch house. She bumped up against whoever stood most apart from the crowd. Once that person moved in, she chose the next candidate. When she had everyone crowded into a corner of the patio, the revelers noticed they had been herded. Fascinated, they spread back out and watched as Blue diligently and enthusiastically herded them again. Her performance was impressive party entertainment, which <u>made Chance as proud as a dad whose kid had hit a home run</u>.

Although that is a Blue success story, the prospect of Blue rounding up Roscoe is slim. *I hope Roscoe doesn't take you seriously and kick you in the head.*

* * *

(7)   Later, Chance heads to the clubhouse to help his dad prepare lunch for the hunters. He gets paid for helping out. Blue is nowhere to be seen. <u>Chance observes riders sweep past Roscoe in the south pasture, led by baying hounds hot after their prey.</u>

(8)   As he approaches the clubhouse, he notices one of the fancy women making a <u>gallant</u> effort to corral a litter of tiny puppies running amuck. "Can I hold one?" he asks.

"Sure." The lady picks up the runt of the litter. "His name is Biscuit."

The pup licks and nuzzles, wags and wiggles. Chance doesn't want to give him up, but his dad needs help with lunch, so after a few minutes, he hands Biscuit back.

The lady smiles and reaches out to shake Chance's hand. No woman has ever done that before. He awkwardly takes it and thanks her, calling her "ma'am" as his father, <u>a gentleman cowboy</u>, had taught him.

(9)   Not long after, he is in the clubhouse stuffing bottles of <u>Mexican</u> beer into a tub of ice. His dad comes in. <u>Two ranch hands trail behind but stop just inside the door.</u>

"Son," Dad says, <u>putting his hand on Chance's shoulder</u>, "Blue is gone."

"What do you mean *gone*?"

"The hounds lost the coyote's trail. Blue was in the area. She ran, and they zeroed in on her. She's gone, Buddy."

<u>Chance glances at the ranch hands who shade their eyes behind brims of cowboy hats and shift their weight from side to side.</u> Dad <u>pats Chance's shoulder</u> and heads

back outside, <u>his head low and his stride lacking its usual energetic gait. The ranch hands tip their hats and follow. Chance stares for a moment at the empty space they leave before</u> he resumes cramming beer into the ice-filled tub. A tear drops onto his hand. *Those goddamned rich people and their <u>sonsabitchen</u>, stupid-ass dogs.*

(10) Chance struggles through the day, setting up tables and chairs and helping serve food. Afterward, he's cleaning up when his dad approaches.

"Go home, son. We'll take it from here."

<u>Ranch hands watch as</u> Chance slinks away. <u>Rich people lower their heads. Some look away.</u>

* * *

(11) After slamming the front door and marching to his room, Chance flings himself on<u>to</u> his bed and sobs ~~uncontrollably~~. He remembers how Blue would bound onto the bed to comfort him when he felt bad. <u>She would circle around, nudge him, lick his face, and plunk down next to him, her breath on his face and the pressure of her chin on his shoulder. He would pull her close, aware of the softness of her coat and the warmth of her body.</u> *Oh, god, she's gone. My Blue is gone. Oh, god.*

(12) It is late afternoon when Dad comes home, carrying containers of leftovers. He wakes Chance from a fitful sleep. "This may sound strange, Buddy, but the dog's owners want to give you a puppy. I'll understand if you don't want that. It's little consolation and probably too soon, but the offer was made."

Chance's throat tightens. <u>He can hardly breathe. His voice is scratchy.</u> "I don't want it."

"Probably a good call." His dad pats him on the thigh and leaves. Chance hears the rich men's trucks rumble down the road—their dogs howling—<u>and presses a pillow over his head.</u>

* * *

(13)   Several months later, Chance helps with a hunt for the first time since he lost Blue. Back home, afterward, he helps his dad load the freezer with leftovers. Someone knocks at the door, and the woman who shook his hand enters holding a dog. Chance doesn't move. <u>He cannot move.</u> She holds the pup out to him. "It's Biscuit," she said. "<u>He's my favorite.</u> I saved him for you."

The pup squirms and <u>stretches out to Chance,</u> kicking furiously, trying to free himself from her grasp. Chance still can't move. The lady puts the dog down. He circles Chance and jumps up, begging for a pick up. Chance looks at the lady. Her eyes are misty. He looks at his dad, who is also misty-eyed. Biscuit is going nuts. Finally, Chance picks him up. "He's pretty healthy for being a runt," he says.

"He's a good dog, and he has your name written all over him," Dad says.

Biscuit wags his tail frantically, licks Chance's face, and bites at his ear. <u>He burrows his nose into Chance's neck briefly, sneezes, and explores the rest of his face.</u> Biscuit's whole body is churning. The dog is beside himself.

Chance laughs, which increases Biscuit's excitement. "Yep. I'll take him."

"He's yours," the lady says and reaches out her hand for a handshake.

Excitement churns in Chance's stomach. "Thank you, ma'am. <u>Thank you.</u>"

(14) <u>"Would you like to stay for supper?" Dad asks the lady.</u>

<u>"Sure. I'll help." She and Dad head to the kitchen.</u>

The screen door slams as Chance heads outside to romp with Biscuit. *Maybe rich people aren't so bad after all.*

Story Autopsy of "Rich Man's Sport"

(1) The first paragraph does substantial work.
- The writing is economical while being rich with innuendo and detail. Every word conveys information. Intriguing information is designed to grab the reader.
- Reveals the **point of view** from which the story is told—third person limited.
- Establishes **tense**—present tense.
- Reveals **setting** (time, place, environment).
- Introduces the **main character** (suggests age, his western/country culture, and his opinion of "fancy" women).
- Incorporates **action** into the scene.
- Notes an **inciting incident** to come, a hunt.
- Creates **curiosity** by hinting at the upcoming event.
- Implies a **key situation** (Mom and Dad are separated).
- Suggests **conflict** and **tension** between cultures.

(2) The second paragraph builds on the first one.
- Introduces **supporting character**, Blue.
- Expands on **setting** details.
- Introduces "the hunt."
- Hints at **theme**—boy/dog relationship and boy evolving.
- Keeps **character development** and **descriptive details** economical so they don't slow the pace of the story.

(3) Historical details are revealed.
- Reveals that Mom left—a **defining moment.**
- Suggests **tension/conflict** between Mom's world and Dad's (Dad's "old" truck versus Mom's city world).
- Gives more details about Blue and how Chance got her. Shows generosity of the (rich) ranch owner.

- Note intentional **tense change** done without jolting the reader: "Blue *was* a puppy when . . . "
- Reveals Chance's dreams and thoughts, which provide details about the **culture** in which he lives.
- Reveals more cultural details that would have interrupted **flow** if described earlier.

(4) Contrasts Chance's low opinion of rich people and the fox hunt with his affection for dogs.

(5) Dad is introduced as a supporting character.
  - *Cowboy-like* implies a lot about Dad.
  - Hints at father/son **relationship**—affectionate slap on the head demonstrates Dad's playfulness.
  - Shows Dad's occupation and sense of humor. Promotes his likability factor.

(6) Details of the boy's history and his relationship with his dog are revealed.
  - Describes the **main character**, Chance, in more detail.
  - Shares his thoughts in italics.
  - Reveals the depth of the boy/dog relationship.

(7) The stage is set for drama to come.
  - **Foreshadows** a key event to come (Blue's demise) without giving it away. (Hint: Once an ending is determined, go back and foreshadow it without giving it away.)

(8) The story moves along and sets up the climax.
  - Setting changes to the clubhouse (* * *).
  - Introduces **dialogue.**
  - Introduces another **key character**—a "fancy" woman.

- Introduces a dog, Biscuit. Giving the dog a name suggests his importance.
- The lady doesn't quite fit Chance's opinion of rich women.
- Her shaking his hand surprises him—shows respect he didn't expect and had not experienced before.
- Defines Dad as a "gentleman cowboy," which makes him likable. Shows Chance has internalized that image.
- Emphasizes Chance's affection for dogs.

(9) An all-important turning point in the story is revealed, which includes a shock factor—Blue is gone.

- This profound and **unusual event** keeps the middle from slumping.
- The **bond between men** who work together as ranch hands is demonstrated, not through words, but by their presence and the hat-tipping gesture.
- Shows Chance's deep **emotional response** (he is stunned) to what has happened—the tear on his hand and his staring at the empty space left by the ranch hands (*show, don't tell*) reflects a **defining moment**.
- The **unexpected** adult swear words from the young boy reveal the intensity of his emotions and suggest his exposure to the rowdy, adult ranch-hand culture.

(10) Chance tries to "cowboy up" and be tough. He carries on until Dad releases him.

- Again, ranch hands stand with Chance. They are attentive and compassionate in their own subtle way.
- Awkwardness of the "rich" people suggests compassion.
- The **setting changes** back to the bunkhouse (* * *).

(11) The depth of Chance's emotions are exposed.

- Removing the adverb, *uncontrollably*, lets the strong verb, *sobs*, speak for itself, and gives it greater impact.
- Reveals **history** and intensity of boy/dog relationship.

(12) A low point is established before the resolution.
- Rich people try to make it right.
- Dad's intuitiveness is revealed—it's too soon.
- Dad's likability factor continues to increase—the pat on the thigh is a manly, affectionate act.
- The pillow over Chance's head shows the level of hurt and bitterness.
- Readers may envision the lady in one of those trucks and her emotions.
- **Scene break** and **time lapse**—months later (* * *).

(13) A resolution is best executed with staccato hits of action and information.
- Chance is back at work and rallying.
- The lady and the dog reappear.
- This evokes strong **emotions** in Chance. He can hardly move, breathe, or talk.
- Biscuit sells the deal—he's all over it (the irresistible nuzzle and sneeze).
- Chance softens—he **changes.**
- Again, the lady offers a handshake. It seems more natural to Chance this time and creates a connection.

(14) The dénouement (the final part of the story after the resolution) gives readers satisfaction.
- **Surprise.** Do the fancy lady and dad have something going on? This implies both past collaboration and future consequences.
- The screen door slamming is reflective of the rural bunkhouse setting.
- Chance and the dog are off—together.
- Chance has **changed.** His opinion of "rich people" has softened.
- The reader is given a **satisfactory ending.**

RECOMMENDED READINGS

On Writing Well by William Zinsser
On Writing: A Memoir of the Craft by Stephen King
bird by bird by Anne Lamott
The Red Sneaker Writers Series by William Bernhardt:
    Sizzling Style, Powerful Premise, Excellent Editing,
    Dynamic Dialogue, Creating Character, Perfecting
    Plot, Story Structure, Thinking Theme
Tell It Slant by Brenda Miller and Suzanne Paola
Story Masters by William Kessler
Story Genius and *Wired for Story* by Lisa Cron
The Everything Guide to Writing Nonfiction by Richard D. Bank
Crafting the Personal Essay: A Guide for Writing and
    Publishing Creative Nonfiction by Dinty W. Moore
Writing Active Setting by Mary Buckham
Scene & Structure by Jack Bickham
Characters & Viewpoint by Orson Scott Card
It was the "best" of sentences, it was the "worst" of
    sentences. by June Casagrande
Sin and Syntax by Constance Hale
Word Up! by Marcia Riefer Johnston
All in a Word: 100 Delightful Excursions into the Uses and
    Abuses of Words by Vivian Cook
Getting the Words Right by Theodore A. Rees Cheney
Reading Like a Writer by Francine Prose
Water for Elephants by Sara Gruen (prologue example)
Saints, Unexpected by Brent van Staalduinen (where to
    start a story)
Joe, the Slave Who Became an Alamo Legend by
    Ron J. Jackson and Lee Spencer White (example of
    how to fill in historical blanks)
Me Talk Pretty One Day by David Sedaris (examples of
    vignettes and creating comedic stories out of tidbits)

Reference Guides (Style Books)

The Elements of Style by William Strunk, Jr., and E. B. White (A pocket-size version is available on Amazon)

The Chicago Manual of Style is used mostly by novelists and their editors. (It's expensive, but a laminated cheat-sheet version is available on Amazon.)

The Associated Press Stylebook is used mostly by journalists. (This is available on Amazon.)

Recommended Sources of Writing Information

100 Writing Mistakes to Avoid by Maeve Maddox

The Only Grammar Book You'll Ever Need by Susan Thurman

Writers Write by Amanda Patterson

The Writer magazine (resource for writing information and for keeping up to date with the publishing industry)

BrainyQuote by Amanda Patterson (an online source of writer information and quotes)

The Emotion Thesaurus by Angela Ackerman and Becca Puglisi

The Artful Edit by Susan Bell

—Be a Reader.—

INDEX

WORKSHOPS AND PRESENTATIONS
BY NIKKI HANNA

LISTEN UP, WRITER
A Series on How *Not* to Write Like an Amateur

Find Joy and Purpose in Writing—Encourages writers to take a fresh look at why they write and to develop a definition of success that taps into innate talents and that is achievable.

Tap into Craft—The Road to Authorship—Reveals common craft mistakes writers make—the ones that shout *amateur.*

Get the Most Out of Revision, Editing, and Proofing—Ensures a writer produces work that is impressive enough to compete in the writing marketplace.

Nail the Structure—Beginnings, Endings, and In-Between—Covers how to write compelling beginnings and endings and how to keep the middle from slumping.

Write with Voice, Style, and Humor—Shows writers how to find personal voice and style so the writing stands out from that of other writers, delights readers, and impresses publishers.

Capture Life through Memoir—Writing the Hard Stuff—Shows how to write a captivating life story, how to write about difficult times and flawed characters, how to decide what to put in and what to leave out, and how to print and publish.

Create Compelling Nonfiction—Covers writing principles that apply to various categories of nonfiction (biography/memoir, instructional, self-help, essay, inspirational, illustrative). Writing tips that apply to other genres and publishing options are included.

Apply Winning Strategies to Writing Contests—Demonstrates how to be more competitive in contests and how to strategically select them. Key tips increase the odds of winning.

Evaluate Printing, Publishing, and Marketing Options—Discloses nuances of the industry and describes the pros and cons of various publishing strategies so writers can make sound, informed decisions.

neqhanna@sbcglobal.net - www.nikkihanna.com

BOOKS BY NIKKI HANNA

Available on Amazon, Kindle, and at www.nikkihanna.com

OUT OF IOWA INTO OKLAHOMA
You Can Take the Girl Out of Iowa, but
You Can't Take the Iowa Out of the Girl

CAPTURE LIFE—WRITE A MEMOIR
Create a Life Story—Leave a Legacy

WRITE WHATEVER THE HELL YOU WANT
Finding Joy and Purpose in Writing

RED HEELS & SMOKIN'
How I Got My Moxie Back

NEAR SEX EXPERIENCES
A Woman in Crescendo, Aging with Bravado

HEY, KIDS, WATCH THIS
Go BEYOND Aging Well

LEADERSHIP SAVVY
How to Stand Out as a Leader, Promote Employee
Loyalty, and Build an Energized Workforce

LISTEN UP, WRITER
How *Not* to Write Like an Amateur—The Path
to Authorship

neqhanna@sbcglobal.net - www.nikkihanna.com

ABOUT THE AUTHOR

When asked to describe herself in one sentence, Nikki Hanna said, "I'm a metropolitan gal who never quite reached the level of refinement and sophistication that label implies." The contradictions reflected in this description are the basis for much of her humorous prose. She describes her writing as irreverent and quirky with strong messages.

As an author, writing coach, and writing contest judge, Hanna is dedicated to inspiring others. She speaks on writing and offers writing workshops on the craft of writing, memoir writing, writing contest strategy, writing with voice/style/humor, finding joy and purpose in writing, and other writing topics. She also speaks on aging, leadership, and women's issues.

In addition to numerous awards for poetry, essays, books, and short stories, Hanna received the Oklahoma Writers' Federation, Inc.'s *Crème de la Crème* Award and Rose State College's Outstanding Writer Award. As a self-published writer, her book awards include the National Indie Excellence Award, the USA Best Book Finalist Award, two International Book Excellence Awards, and four Independent Book Awards. Her books are available on Amazon and through her website.

Hanna has a BS degree in business education and journalism and an MBA from the University of Tulsa. A retired CPA and Toastmaster, her years of experience in management and as an executive for one of the country's largest companies fostered a firm grip on leadership. She also served as a consultant on national industry task forces, as a board member for corporations, and as an advisor on curriculum development and strategic planning for educational institutions and charity organizations.

Hanna lives in Tulsa, Oklahoma. Her children decided she had become a bit of a pistol in her old age after she and her sixty-something friends were banned from a sushi bar for a food fight. The kids tell her, "Don't call me if you get thrown in jail." Four grandchildren consider her the toy fairy, and those in California believe she lives at the airport.

Made in the USA
Columbia, SC
11 March 2020

88996265R00152